LOTUS 49

© Haynes Publishing 2014

Ian Wagstaff has asserted his right to be identified
as the author of this work.

First published in November 2014

All rights reserved. No part of this publication may be
reproduced or stored in a retrieval system or transmitted,
in any form or by any means, electronic, mechanical,
photocopying, recording or otherwise, without prior
permission in writing from Haynes Publishing.

A catalogue record for this book is available
from the British Library

ISBN 978 0 85733 412 1

Library of Congress control no. 2014935022

Published by Haynes Publishing,
Sparkford, Yeovil, Somerset BA22 7JJ, UK
Tel: 01963 442030 Fax: 01963 440001
Int. tel: +44 1963 442030 Int. fax: +44 1963 440001
E-mail: sales@haynes.co.uk
Website: www.haynes.co.uk

Haynes North America Inc.
861 Lawrence Drive, Newbury Park,
California 91320, USA

Printed in the USA by Odcombe Press LP,
1299 Bridgestone Parkway, La Vergne, TN 37086

LOTUS 49

1967–1970 (all marks)

Owners' Workshop Manual

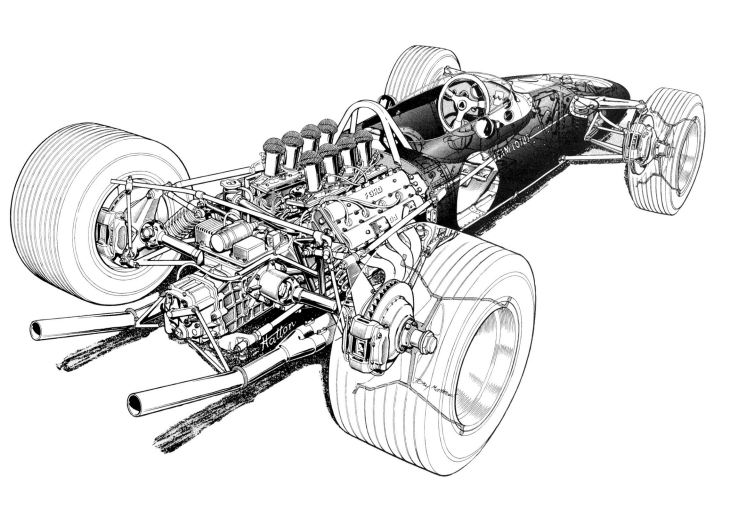

An insight into the design, engineering, maintenance
and operation of the ground-breaking Lotus Formula 1 car

Ian Wagstaff

Contents

Introduction

During my research for this book I was reminded that I still had a poster from the 1969 British Grand Prix at Silverstone. It is from a different world. The entrance fee was 17/6d in advance (between £12 and £13 at today's prices), or £1 on the day, with children getting in for 5/- and car parking free. Greed had yet to become an integral part of Formula 1. Yet there is something in the poster that heralded change. It is dominated by a drawing of the reigning champions, the Lotus-Cosworth 49 and Graham Hill. Like any 1969 grand prix contender, the car in the drawing features a wing and is adorned in a sponsor's livery. Two seasons earlier, the Lotus 49, like virtually every racing car before it, would have been devoid of aerodynamic aids and would have been painted in its national colour scheme.

As the first car designed to make use of the 3-litre Cosworth DFV engine and the last to be used by a privateer to win a World Championship grand prix, the Lotus 49 has an undoubted place in history but, more than that, it is an indicator of how, after around six decades, the face of grand prix racing had dramatically changed. A simple design, the 49 chassis with its DFV engine was a package that defined a formula, and the Cosworth power unit became the most successful in grand prix history.

The Lotus 49 story is not just about the car's technical merits but also about some of the leading figures of motor racing history, including Lotus founder Colin Chapman, Cosworth designer Keith Duckworth and Jim Clark, perhaps the greatest of all post-war racing drivers. Graham Hill took the World Championship at the wheel of a 49, and in all there were to be five World Champions among the 49's factory drivers. One grey Friday at Donington Park in 2007 I saw for myself just what the car meant to one of those World Champions, Mario Andretti, from the delight on his face when he was reunited with a Lotus 49.

Acknowledgements

As with the first title in this series, the *Lotus 72 Manual*, the following pages would have been impossible to write without the kind and thorough assistance of Classic Team Lotus at Hethel. My particular thanks go to Clive Chapman, Colin's son, who heads the operation, to merchandising and events coordinator Sapphire Whitbread and to Kevin Smith who was responsible for the rebuild of R2/R11.

Among the drivers consulted, Emerson Fittipaldi and Tony Trimmer appear for the third time in this series. My thanks to them and also to Jackie Oliver, Mario Andretti, Richard Attwood and John Miles for their recollections, and also to Brian Redman, who so nearly drove a 49, and to Sean Walker, whose experience of the car was simply along the runway at Hethel but who was able to confirm what his late father, Ian, had once told me about the origins of the Gold Leaf sponsorship.

The former Lotus mechanics – 'the Vicar', 'Joe 90', 'Beaky', 'Buckshot' *et al* – are a great bunch to talk to and, for this work, I must express my appreciation to Bob Dance (and his little black book), Tony Cleverly, Eddie Dennis, Dave Lazenby, Allan McCall, Derek Mower, Dale Porteous, Dick Scammell, Dave Sims, Bob Sparshott and Leo Wybrott.

From those who continue to cherish, race or still work on the Lotus 49, I must acknowledge the help given by Geoff Farmer (the present owner of chassis R7), Chris MacAllister (who still races R2/R11), Joaquin Folch-Rusiñol, Simon Hadfield (Simon Hadfield Motorsports), Doug Hill and Ian Stanfield (National Motor Museum), and Christopher Tate and Gary Rankin (Donington Collection).

Others to thank include Mike Costin (the 'Cos' of Cosworth and the first man ever to drive a Lotus 49), James Knight (Bonhams), Jeff Bloxham, Sally Swart, Andy Brown, Stephen Slater, William Hewland, Wayne Collins, John Nicholson, John Waghorn, Stephanie Sykes (BRDC library), Dave Hill (Ford Photographic), Ted Walker (Ferret Fotographics), David Pearson (Motoprint), John Lacko, Sutton Images, LAT and my indefatigable editor, Steve Rendle.

Many books and periodicals were referred to and, in particular, I must acknowledge the scholarship of Michael Oliver, Doug Nye and the late David Hodges. I hope that Michael, author of the definitive *Lotus 49 – The Story of a Legend*, did not mind the occasional phone call. I never did get to the bottom of whether they were peaches or oranges in the Douglas DC3 to Sao Paulo.

Ian Wagstaff May 2014

'Twice the horsepower of most
Formula 1 cars I have driven before.'

Jim Clark
Team Lotus driver

Chapter One

The Lotus 49 story

There was nothing really innovative in the Lotus 49. It was a basic car, built to carry the new Cosworth DFV engine. It was, however, immediately successful – Jim Clark won its first ever race – and it went on to epitomise the early years of the 3-litre formula. It took Graham Hill to the 1968 World Championship and assisted in Jochen Rindt's posthumous 1970 title.

OPPOSITE The start of the 1967 British Grand Prix at Silverstone, with the two Lotus 49s of Jim Clark (left) and Graham Hill blasting away from the front of the grid. *(Ford)*

The Return of Power

RAC British Grand Prix
SPONSORED BY
DAILY MAIL

3

Brands Hatch 16th July 1966

official programme

he new formula for 1966 was heralded as 'The Return of Power'. After five years of racing tiny 1½-litre projectiles, Formula 1 would be back where it belonged, featuring powerful, bulky cars with engines now twice the size of their immediate predecessors. Although there was plenty of warning of this change, initially it looked as if the *garagistes* – Enzo Ferrari's scornful tag for the small British teams that had come to the fore in grand prix racing – would be caught out again, unprepared as they had been when the formula had last changed half a decade earlier.

Back in 1960, the final year of the 2½-litre

formula, the British had headed the field. For 1961 they took one look at the proposed 1½-litre formula, decided that the cars would hardly be worth the name of Formula 1 and, Luddite-like, put their faith in an alternative 3-litre 'Intercontinental Formula'. It failed to attract much overseas attention and, in 1961, the well-prepared Ferrari team almost swept the F1 World Championship. Only the genius of Stirling Moss prevented Ferrari from doing so totally.

It was almost the same in 1966, despite the fact that the British now had their wish of larger engines and plenty of notice of the change, the FIA's rule-making body, the Commission Sportive Internationale (CSI), having announced the move to a 3-litre formula in 1963. At the start of 1966, a miscellany of ideas was on the table but again it appeared that Ferrari was more ready than most, with a 3-litre V12 engine using know-how from sportscar racing. The fact that Ferrari did not win the World Championship that year had little to do with anything technical and a lot to do with politics, to whit the antagonism between John Surtees and Ferrari team manager Eugenio Dragoni that led to Surtees' departure from the team before mid-season.

The simplicity of Repco's V8 won out in the end in 1966, but it would not be until the following year that the British teams found a long-term answer to their engine conundrums in the form of the Cosworth DFV. This Ford-backed V8 would go on to become the most successful grand prix engine of all time, eventually powering many of the

teams. However, during its first season it was exclusively used in the car with which it will always be best remembered – the Lotus 49.

A hotchpotch of ideas

There was no agreement as to what engine configuration would be best at the start of the 1966 season. Coventry Climax, which had provided the British teams with grand prix-winning engines for so long, had declared early in 1965 that it would be withdrawing from the sport. The teams scrabbled round for answers and came up with a wide variety.

Repco was confined to what seemed, at the time, an insufficient eight cylinders (in V formation) because of its basis in an Oldsmobile power unit. Ferrari, as mentioned, went for a V12. Cooper also made use of a V12 but this was an elderly Maserati design dating back to 1957. Other V12s were those of Honda and Eagle, the latter's engine a creation of Harry Weslake. McLaren oscillated between the Ford V8 Indy engine and a similarly configured unit from Serenissima. BRM seemed very futuristic with its complicated 16-cylinder H16 engine, but there were many who doubted the existence of the H16 until it appeared.

ABOVE Some, including Ferrari, thought 12 cylinders was the way to go for the 3-litre formula. This is Chris Amon in 1967. *(Author)*

LEFT For the more impoverished teams, there was always the four-cylinder Coventry Climax FPF, which dated back to the 2½-litre Formula 1 of 1954 to 1960. Former motorcycle racer Bob Anderson was one who used such an engine in his Brabham BT11. *(Author)*

One weekly motor racing newspaper, perhaps overcome with the potential excitement, reported on the possibility of an engine of 'X32' configuration from the Far East!

There were also those who relied on enlarged engines from previous formulae, either because they were waiting for something else to turn up or because they just did not have the wherewithal for anything different. So it was that 2.7-litre four-cylinder Coventry Climax units dating back to 1960 and bored-out 2-litre BRM and Climax V8s from the 1961–65 era could be found on the grids, even into 1967. For teams forced to use such engines it was all very unsatisfactory. Lotus was one such. There was something waiting in the wings but throughout 1966 Lotus had to make do with the small Climax and BRM V8s or the overly complex BRM H16 that was available for use following an agreement with the arch-rival from Bourne.

Although Jim Clark won the 1966 US Grand Prix with an H16-engined Lotus 43, this was never going to be a long-term relationship.

ABOVE From left, Bill Brown, Keith Duckworth, Mike Costin and Ben Rood with their new creation, the DFV. *(Ford)*

RIGHT As well as the DFV, Ford agreed to fund the 1.6-litre FVA Formula 2 engine for 1967. *(Ford)*

But Colin Chapman had already sounded out Cosworth and found funding from Ford for what was to become the DFV V8. For such a new, untried power unit, Lotus would have to start with a straightforward car that could at least serve while the DFV found its feet, but the new 49 was an immediate success and for several years there was no need to look further. In that first season, with the DFV mounted on to the rear bulkhead of the 49's monocoque, it was almost as if engine and car were as one.

The DFV was the first Formula 1 engine from Cosworth, the company founded by Keith Duckworth and Mike Costin. Chapman brought together Duckworth and Ford, in the persons of public affairs director Walter Hayes and director of engineering Harley Copp, the result being that Ford agreed to fund the 3-litre DFV engine and the 1.6-litre FVA Formula 2 engine for a mere £100,000. Prior to this point Duckworth had never designed a grand prix engine.

The DFV (Double Four Valve) was a 90° V8 initially rated at 400bhp. For such a new engine,

Chapman decided that he needed a simple car, one in which the engine could be used as a stressed part of the chassis. Chapman and Maurice Phillippe, therefore, created a design evolved from the H16-engined Lotus 43, the first Lotus in which the engine was bolted to the back of the hull and the suspension secured to the back of the engine.

The resulting Lotus 49 was attractive in its simplicity. By the middle of May 1967 the first example had been tested by Graham Hill, who had returned to the team after seven years at BRM; the first person ever to drive a Type 49, however, was Costin. Come the end of the month, two cars were ready to enter the Dutch Grand Prix, the third round of the World Championship. Lotus drivers Jim Clark and Hill were already well behind Brabham's Denny Hulme in the World Championship, which Clark had won in 1963 and 1965, and Hill in 1962. Clark had yet to score, while Hill had six points following his second place at Monaco in the little 2-litre Lotus-BRM 33.

LEFT **The prototype Lotus 49, R1, as seen in public for the first time.** *(Ford)*

THE 1967 DUTCH GRAND PRIX

Jim Clark had not even seen a Lotus 49 when he arrived at Zandvoort in June 1967. Graham Hill had already tested the new contender so perhaps it was not surprising that he was the one who planted it on pole position and then led for the first 10 laps of the Dutch Grand Prix. Team Lotus itself had not been that confident and, just in case, had brought along as a spare a 2-litre BRM-engined Type 33, a leftover from the previous formula.

The Lotus 49 looked good from the outset. Towards the end of the first day of practice, Hill opened up and set the fastest lap with 49/R1. Clark, by contrast, felt that all was not right with the handling of 49/R2. Nothing was obviously amiss but the taper roller front wheel bearings, being new, were thought to need adjustment. Before the next day's practice R1's steering and suspension were carefully checked and slight play in the front

wheel ball-races found. Practice had barely begun when a ball-race in the right rear hub broke up and split the hub carrier. It was the beginnings of this that the astute Clark had felt the previous day. At first a design failure was suspected but the ball-race itself proved to be faulty.

While a new hub assembly was fitted to his car, Clark could only watch as Hill maintained his grip of the fastest lap. Then an electrical fault occurred on Hill's car: perhaps these new 49s were fragile – at least that was what some increasingly unhappy rivals were hoping. Problem cured, Hill put in some fast laps, his final one given officially as a jaw-dropping 1min 24.6sec. There were those who said it had been 'only' 1min 25.0sec but even that would have been good enough for pole. The opposition was reported as appearing 'bewildered'. Clark, his car ready to go again, had time for a few laps, although not enough to show a real turn of speed. The Team Lotus mechanics set about an all-nighter to check the rear hub assemblies.

It could be said that the 3-litre Formula 1 era truly began at 2.30pm the next day. Under a grey sky, and with a typically strong wind from the North Sea blowing across the seaside circuit, 17 cars moved up from a dummy grid. Clark somehow eased himself from the third row into the second. An unwise official noted Pedro Rodriguez's Cooper-Maserati was also

creeping forward and wandered among the cars trying to point out the error of the Mexican's ways.

Hill led away, closely pursued by a five-car tail, at the end of which was Clark, still learning what the Lotus 49 was all about, a task not made easier by the fact that different rear springs and rear tyres had been fitted since practice. With five laps gone, Hill appeared to be in complete command with a 2sec lead over Jack Brabham's Brabham-Repco. Meanwhile, Clark was, in effect, still practising.

The lead gap remained about the same until lap 10, but the next time the start-line crowd saw Hill he was jogging behind his 49 as the mechanics pushed it to the Team Lotus pit. Hill put a mutually sympathetic arm around designer Keith Duckworth. A camshaft drive gear wheel had broken. That was the bad news, but the good news was that Clark reckoned he had done sufficient practice and it was time to go racing.

Within five laps Clark overtook the man who would later score the Lotus 49's last win, Jochen Rindt in a Cooper-Maserati, for second place. Now only Jack Brabham stood in Clark's way and he was despatched the following lap. Clark then pulled away in seemingly effortless fashion and by half distance his performance was being described as 'devastating'. Driver and car were as one while the new Cosworth DFV in R2 was not missing a beat. With no idea what had happened to Hill, Clark could just pray that the same problem would not put him out of the race. Nothing occurred and with 90 laps finished and the chequered flag out, he pulled in to a rapturous welcome from his team. Those members of the Ford (England) top brass present could allow themselves a smile of satisfaction. Their money had already been well spent. After the race it was found that Clark's engine had a cracked timing gear, due to torsional vibration at low revs.

In World Championship history this was only the third time that an all-new car, one that was different in design from stem to stern, had won its first grand prix. Only the Maserati 250F and Mercedes-Benz W196 had previously achieved this.

Fast but fragile

The two new Lotus 49s made their début at Zandvoort. Both led the race and Clark's won it, Hill having to retire. Such is the stuff of legend, although Duckworth felt that a fair amount of luck had been involved in getting one of his new DFVs to the end.

In one move Lotus now had the most competitive car in the paddock to add to the world's best driver. The 1967 Lotus 49, however, was not the most reliable car. Although there would be further grand prix wins that year, there would be no World Championship to add to the début victory, at least not that season.

For the Belgian Grand Prix at Spa, Clark took pole and sailed off into the distance in the opening laps, only to have to pit twice with spark-plug maladies. The mechanics were initially accused of over-tightening them, but this was incorrect. Hill fared rather worse for his engine died on the grid and then, shortly after he got going, his clutch failed. It was the type of race that loses World Championships.

On, then, to France and the Le Mans Bugatti circuit, an unloved venue that seemed mainly to occupy the car parks used for the 24-hour race. Attention from an over-zealous customs official meant that Lotus missed early practice, and then fuel injection problems led to misfiring when the 49s did get going. Despite all this, Hill was able to snatch pole at the last moment. Both he and Clark were among the early leaders before retiring with transmission problems. Memories of the dream début were receding fast.

The ZF gearboxes in the 49s were strengthened for the next round of the championship. Team Lotus was now on home ground, Silverstone, and again there were misfiring problems during practice. Once those were solved, Clark put his car on pole and Hill joined him on the front row. However, suspension failure on Hill's car towards the end of practice resulted in a seemingly catastrophic accident as he headed for the pits.

The wreck was returned to Hethel where everyone – with the exception of mechanic Allan McCall, who was left at Brackley to prepare Clark's car – set about rebuilding it for

ABOVE The mechanics worked miracles to get Hill on to the grid for the 1967 British Grand Prix. A one-off replacement nose made his car look more like a Lotus 33 at the front. *(Ford)*

BELOW Home run. Clark won again at Silverstone in 1967. Maurice Phillippe, Keith Duckworth, Hughie Absalom, Gordon Huckle and Dick Scammell were among those on the victory trailer. *(Author)*

the following day. The result was the ultimate all-nighter and when Hill's car was wheeled on to the grid the next day mechanics were still working on it. With a cobbled-together aluminium nose (rather than a glass-fibre one) made from an early buck and an earlier-style windscreen, the front of the car somewhat resembled an old Lotus 33.

Early in the race it looked as if all the effort was worth it. While Clark led, Hill initially followed in second place, then lost out to Brabham for a while, then regained second place as he got used to the rebuilt car. For a while the two 49s ran round in formation before Hill eventually slipped into the lead. On lap 55, a missing Allen screw from a top transverse suspension link sent Hill into the pits. He returned to the race only to suffer engine failure nine laps later. Meanwhile, Clark had the race easily in hand and took a comfortable win.

Practice for the German Grand Prix was sometimes fraught and Hill crashed again. Eventually, though, Clark set an emphatic pole-winning time. Although he took the initial lead, collapsed suspension brought an early end to his race. Hill's nightmare continued as well that day. The Lotus 49s were obviously quick but were they strong enough?

For the first time, Canada was to have a round of the World Championship. It was not uncommon for Chapman to enter a third car for a local driver, particularly when far from home and in this case Eppie Wietzes, who was more used to a Ford GT40, was assigned the prototype R1, which Clark damaged during an early practice session, meaning that repairs were needed before the Canadian could get behind the wheel.

Clark and Hill took the first two positions on the grid, Hill doing well considering that he was suffering from flu. Under drizzling conditions on race day it was decided to start the Lotuses on wet Firestone tyres whereas the Brabham team chose intermediates, and consequently the lead fluctuated as the conditions changed. Eventually the rain got the better of the electrics in Clark's car, as well as in Wietzes's. Hill had a far from comfortable day but kept going to come fourth and post his maiden finish in a 49.

The circus popped back to Europe for the Italian Grand Prix, where Giancarlo Baghetti was offered what was to be his last World Championship race in the third Type 49. For Hill, the Monza race brought another retirement, this time, like Baghetti, with engine failure. For Clark, however, this was to be one of his greatest races, but one with scant reward – fourth place.

Clark set another pole but he was caught out by a mix-up at the start and it was not until lap three that he took the lead. He was experiencing handling problems, however, and he was not aware of the reason until Jack Brabham, following a brave move, was able to come alongside and signal that the Lotus had a puncture. Following a pit stop Clark returned in 15th place – and now began what would be regarded as one of his greatest drives. So far during 1967 he had seemed to be driving within himself, but now he raced with a vengeance.

He took just 10 laps to catch the tail of the leading trio, which was still a lap ahead of him and included team-mate Hill. The next step was to unlap himself. Not long after, Hill found himself comfortably in the lead after Denny Hulme's Brabham-Repco suffered a blown head gasket. Meanwhile, Clark was lapping faster than anyone else and was moving further up the field. On lap 59 Hill's crankshaft broke, his engine spectacularly indicating his demise as he

swept into the Parabolica. Shortly after, Clark took both Surtees and Brabham. The incredible had happened: despite having been a lap down, he was back in the lead.

Had the race been one lap shorter, Clark would have achieved one of the most famous of all victories, but as he rounded the Curva Grande for the final time his engine coughed and his two rivals were past. The DFV appeared to be out of fuel, leading to conjecture as to whether the engine had failed to pick up the last couple of gallons or whether there just had not been enough in the tank. Apart from being denied a magnificent win, the result meant that Clark now had no hope of winning the World Championship that year.

The teams returned to the American continent where Clark indicated what could have been by winning in the USA and Mexico, the last two races of the season. He took both

The appearance of the Lotus 49s at the 1968 Spanish Grand Prix in a garish red, white and gold colour scheme seemed to herald in a new era. In truth, it was not the first time a Formula 1 car had appeared in a sponsor's livery. Indeed, it was not even the maiden appearance of the team as Gold Leaf Team Lotus.

Up to the end of the 1950s, sponsors were unknown in Grand Prix racing. A Cooper was simply a Cooper, a BRM was just a BRM, and all the cars, with not a logo to be seen on their flanks, were simply painted in their national colours; for example, green for British entrants, red for Italian and blue for French. Life was simpler and there was considerably less money in the sport. The Americans may have raced brash-liveried cars adorned by sponsors' decals and named after financial benefactors such as Blue Crown Spark Plug or Dean Van Lines but, as far as Europe was concerned, such vulgarity just was not cricket or, to be more precise, not motor racing.

How and why that all changed can be traced back to a meeting that occurred ten years before the advent of Gold Leaf Team Lotus. In 1957 four brothers, the Samengo-Turners, eager to improve the standing of their small company in the then highly competitive world of hire purchase, met with Ken Gregory, team manager of the British Racing Partnership, a motor racing équipe that had come into being early that year and was part owned by Alfred Moss, Stirling's father. Gregory had achieved a reputation for being business savvy in the then arguably naïve world of motor racing, but even he was surprised by what the Samengo-Turners were suggesting. They wanted to give him £40,000 to run his team. In those days, even international teams were financed by start and prize money and by what, by comparison, were pittances from their trade suppliers. Such a sum was unprecedented and would make the team the envy of the paddock. BRP was about to become Yeoman Credit Racing and motor racing would never be quite the same again.

It would not be a smooth path, though, as jealousy, rather than admiration, meant that the establishment sought to destroy BRP rather than follow its lead. It would be almost ten years before the next step was taken.

Former Team Lotus mechanic David Lazenby was running Lotus Components, the commercial side of the racing operation, which in 1967 entered a Lotus 47 sports car for John Miles and Jackie Oliver. Interest was shown by an agent in buying a couple of 47s with the tobacco company John Player possibly involved in the deal. The conversation turned to Formula 1, by which time Lazenby realised that the project might be more than he could cope with and he passed the baton to Team Lotus competitions manager Andrew Ferguson. The result was that a deal was done whereby John Player would sponsor cars under the banner of Gold Leaf Team Lotus.

It seems that the potential of John Player sponsorship came to Colin Chapman's attention

ABOVE There is not a logo in sight on Chris Bristow's Cooper but Yeoman Credit is the sponsor, the first in Formula 1. *(courtesy Ken Gregory)*

RIGHT The fact that motor racing is dangerous was displayed everywhere at race meetings, but not the fact that cigarette smoking is dangerous. This is the outside back cover of the 1968 British Grand Prix programme.

GOLD LEAF TEAM LOTUS is a British motor-racing venture in which Gold Leaf is supporting the engineering brilliance of Lotus-Ford and the driving virtuosity of Graham Hill and Jack Oliver. **Trust GOLD LEAF to taste good**

by more than one route. A friend of Ken Gregory's, and of Chapman's, was Ian Walker, who ran the highly professional Ian Walker Racing, successfully entering Lotus and other cars in lesser formulae. Saddened by the death of some of his drivers, Walker decided to abandon his own team despite the fact that he had been talking to John Player about possible funding and a move up to Formula 1. Rather than just let the matter drop, Walker suggested to Chapman that it might be an idea if he spoke to John Player.

'We weren't very happy about that,' said the then chief mechanic Bob Dance. 'We were Team Lotus; we should be in green and yellow. I figured that we raced [in green] for the country as well as the team. The national colours put an emphasis on it for me, all patriotic stuff. But, as Colin Chapman said, if you lads want a job and to be paid, this is the way forward.'

Racing manager Dick Scammell recalled: 'Colin told us that the cars would have to be red and gold so we painted one up and I looked at it and thought what a Christmas tree that is. I was horrified. I came home and told my wife Frances that it would never last.'

In their last World Championship grand prix in national colours, the Lotus 49s sat on the front row of the grid. Six rows back was a Brabham-Repco BT20 in the orange and brown livery of another tobacco firm, Gunston, driven by South African privateer John Love, who therefore just beat Team Lotus as the first tobacco-sponsored entrant in Formula 1.

The first appearance of the Gold Leaf Lotus 49s was not at a grand prix but at the third round of the 1968 Tasman Series, the Lady Wigram Trophy. The mechanics, having been told news of the sponsorship, had to repaint the cars hastily in a Ford dealership in Christchurch.

Problems with John Player's sailor logo on the side of the cars came to the fore at the first Formula 1 race of the European season, the Race of Champions at Brands Hatch. Graham Hill went out in practice but was black-flagged and not allowed out again until it was covered with masking tape. The sailor was subsequently replaced by a circular Union Jack.

The Gold Leaf colours remained with Team Lotus throughout the rest of the time it raced the Type 49 and during the first season of the 72. In 1972 the red, white and gold livery was replaced by black and gold when the cigarette firm launched its John Player Special brand, and the sponsor also attempted – ultimately without success – to rename the cars 'John Player Specials'.

In 1970, another Lotus 49 team, that of Rob Walker, appeared with a major title sponsor. Not everyone was impressed by this trend. *Motor Sport* magazine's acerbic continental correspondent, Denis Jenkinson, wrote: 'The latest and best giggle in this sponsorship racket, for that is all it is, is "Brooke Bond OXO Racing with Rob Walker". I ask you! Who on earth is going to keep writing that…?'

ABOVE Private owner John Love during a South African Drivers' Championship race at the Roy Hesketh circuit in 1968. The previous year his Team Gunston had become the first Formula 1 entrant to be sponsored by a tobacco company. *(www.motoprint.co.za)*

BELOW The John Player sailor emblem is still apparent on the flanks of Graham Hill's Lotus 49 as Eddie Dennis and Bob Dance push him out for practice at Brands Hatch; soon Hill would be black-flagged and the sailor taped over. *(Author)*

There may have been no title for Team Lotus that year but a Lotus 49 had been on pole position for every championship round since the car had made its début. Despite this, that season's *Autocourse* annual observed, 'Next year both McLaren and the Tyrrell organisations will have Ford engines, so Lotus will have to come up with something better (and stronger) than the 49 if they want to stay in the running.' The writer was about to be proved wrong.

The World Championship year

If ever a season showed great promise for a team, it was 1968. Clark, having won the last two races of the previous year, continued the 49's run of pole positions in South Africa with Graham Hill qualifying second, and that is how they were placed in the race at the end of 80 laps. The Scot had established a new record of 25 grand prix victories and all seemed set for him to repeat his title-winning campaigns of 1963 and '65.

Fitted with 2½-litre versions of the DFV, the Lotus 49s then set off for the Tasman series, held in Australia and New Zealand, resplendent in their traditional green and yellow. They came back, Clark having won the Tasman title, in a gaudy red, white and gold colour scheme. Grand prix cars would never look as attractive again.

Not long after the South African Grand Prix, privateer John Love arranged to buy one of the previous season's 49s, a car with which he would dominate the South African scene for the next couple of years. Rob Walker, arguably the most successful independent of all, also took delivery of the car in which Clark had won at Kyalami. Prospects could not have appeared better.

The first thing to go wrong was the destruction of Rob Walker's new Lotus 49 in a fire. Having been crashed by Jo Siffert in practice for the Race of Champions at Brands Hatch, the car was being stripped down when a spark from a drill set off the conflagration. With Clark's time in England now restricted because of his 'tax-exile' status, the factory only entered Hill for this race and he struggled to find balance during practice. After a lightning start, he then held up a queue of cars before a driveshaft broke. Far worse was to come.

poles as well, with Hill joining him on the front row at Watkins Glen. Another of Chapman's locals, Mexican Moises Solana, joined them for both races. By now it was obvious just how far ahead of the field the Lotus 49 was and the two regular drivers tossed a coin to see who would finish first in the USA. Hill won the toss, an agreement being made that this would mean Clark would take the victory in Mexico. At Watkins Glen, however, an intermittent clutch problem on Hill's car put paid to these best-laid plans and Clark was told to pass his team-mate, who eventually had to ease off. Then, with two and a half laps to go, the top link of Clark's right rear suspension broke and the wheel fell sideways. Most drivers would have abandoned a car in this state by the trackside, but Clark was nevertheless able to keep going and won the race, with a closing Hill in second place.

In Mexico, the 49s again performed well. Indeed, at one point they were first, third and fifth before Solana suffered suspension failure. By the end it seemed like business as usual with Clark winning and Hill dropping out with a broken driveshaft. The situation repeated itself when the season ended with a non-championship race at Jarama, Spain, Clark winning and Hill dropping out with clutch failure.

RIGHT Jim Clark looking forward to the 1968 season in a Gold Leaf-sponsored Lotus 49. Tragically, it was not to be. *(Ford)*

On the first weekend of April, entrant Alan Mann had been hoping that Jim Clark would drive the new Ford P68 sports car in the BOAC endurance race at Brands Hatch, but he was committed to a minor Formula 2 event at Hockenheim. In an accident that has never been fully explained, he left the track on a flat-out right-hand curve, hit a tree and was killed instantly. The effect on the team was naturally devastating and there was even talk that it might pull out of racing.

Perhaps it was Hill, more than anyone else, who pulled Team Lotus together, although at the next non-championship race, the International Trophy at Silverstone, there seemed little appetite for the chase. Despite modifications to the 49, which was now in 49B guise with a Hewland gearbox (see Chapter Two), some of the other manufacturers appeared to be catching up.

Hill was the sole works representative when the World Championship returned to Spain, although Walker had borrowed a factory 49 as a temporary replacement for the one that had been burned out. For the first time, a Lotus 49 was not on pole. In fact Hill was back on the third row, but the final result could not have been a better fillip for the downcast team. Graham fought his way towards the front, taking the lead when Chris Amon's Ferrari retired and then fending off Denny Hulme's McLaren to take the win.

A few days before the Monaco round, Jackie Oliver, who had been driving a Formula 2 car for the factory, found himself promoted into what were surely impossible shoes to fill, those of

BELOW Jackie Oliver's début, at Monaco in 1968, was far from auspicious. *(Ford)*

THE 1968 BRITISH GRAND PRIX

The 1968 British Grand Prix at Brands Hatch was a day of Lotus 49 domination. Only three cars led the race and all of them were 49s – and one of them came first. However, this race has another angle of historical significance: it was the last World Championship grand prix to be won by an independent entry. Nowadays privateers are a thing of the past in Formula 1 and this landmark is likely to stand for good.

The gentlemanly Rob Walker was the ultimate Formula 1 privateer and certainly the most successful. Prior to that day at Brands, his cars had won seven grands prix, an unprecedented number for an independent entrant. His cause had certainly been helped by the fact that in six of those races he had employed the greatest driver of his era – Stirling Moss. However, the French journeyman Maurice Trintignant had also been able to win a grand prix in one of Walker's cars.

Walker first employed Swiss driver Jo Siffert in 1965. In 1966 and '67 they struggled with an overweight Cooper-Maserati, a clutch of fourth places being their best results. But then Walker bought a Lotus 49. His original car, R4, was destroyed by fire after its practice crash at Brands Hatch for the Race of Champions, so Walker ran R2 on loan from the factory until his replacement car, R7, was ready. This was a new 49B and its first race for the team was the 1968 British Grand Prix.

R7 was identical in most respects to the factory cars, although at Brands its wing was lower. At this race Graham Hill ran his usual 49B, R5, while Jackie Oliver had R2, still with a ZF gearbox, to replace the car that he had wrecked at Rouen.

The first practice session saw Oliver use his undoubted local knowledge to overcome the fact that he had an old car while Siffert cautiously learned about his new 49B. A fiery Hill, though, immediately set the pace and by the end of proceedings sat firmly on pole, with Oliver second on the grid and Siffert fourth; only Chris Amon's Ferrari prevented a perfect score.

Twenty minutes before the start of Saturday's race rain began to fall, leading to much dithering about whether to fit rain tyres. Once the flag fell, Oliver led initially but after three laps his team leader moved ahead. Siffert slipped in behind the works Lotus drivers and for over 25 laps the position remained perfect as far as Team Lotus was concerned, with Siffert appearing to be enjoying himself tailing Team Lotus. On lap 26 it started to go wrong for the works cars: Hill turned up the slip road behind the pits with a broken right-hand driveshaft, a rear wheel leaning inwards.

Amon, the only man remotely in contention

LEFT Jo Siffert in the 1968 British Grand Prix in Rob Walker's Lotus 49 – this was the last time a privateer entrant would win a World Championship round. *(Ford)*

with the 49s that weekend, was now harrying Siffert but it looked as if Oliver was about to score his first grand prix victory. Then Amon made a major effort and passed Siffert – perhaps life was not so rosy. Just as Siffert repassed Amon, the final drive unit on Oliver's ZF gearbox gave up at South Bank and suddenly Siffert was in the lead. Once in front there was no way that Siffert, who had already set the day's fastest lap when in third position, would allow the determined Amon to overtake him again, and the Swiss driver duly took victory.

The programme for the meeting contained a full-page advertisement from Rob Walker's Corsley Garage. 'For the man who wants a car that's prepared to be driven hard', ran the slogan. Race winner Siffert had certainly 'driven hard' that day.

Siffert left Walker at the end of 1969, becoming a works driver with March in 1970 and then with BRM in 1971. Driving for BRM in Austria, he scored his second grand prix win. In October of that year he returned to Brands Hatch for the one-off Victory Race, held to celebrate Jackie Stewart's second World Championship title. On lap 15 the spectators in the track's main arena saw a cloud of smoke rising out on the grand prix loop. Siffert's BRM had suffered a suspension failure. The car was pitched across the track with the Swiss driver fatally trapped inside as it rolled over.

BELOW The lap chart of the 1968 British Grand Prix shows the extent of the Lotus 49 domination.

Jim Clark. It did not start well: Monte Carlo was hardly the place to make a grand prix début but Oliver made things worse, upsetting Chapman by bringing a girlfriend with him. Still, a Lotus 49 was back on pole with Hill, and Siffert was third on the grid. Then on the opening lap Oliver, who had been told to take it easy, was unable to take evasive action as an accident happened in front of him. The damage was substantial and Oliver returned to the pits on foot – and was fired. The mechanics still vividly remember the roasting that Chapman handed out. Still, this was Monaco and Hill, having missed out on his two previous visits to the Principality, duly recorded his fourth win there.

With a second place and two wins in the first three rounds of the World Championship, Hill was establishing a tight grip on the title race. If Clark was not there to win the title, then the Londoner was going to get it – but then he failed to score any points in the next four races. More massive efforts on the part of the mechanics ensured that a reinstated Oliver had a 49B for the Belgian Grand Prix, where a combination of officialdom, rain and gearbox maladies saw the two works entries in an unaccustomed place on the penultimate row of the grid. Hill retired with a broken driveshaft universal joint and Oliver nearly went the same way but completed enough laps to finish fifth.

None of the 49s finished in either Holland or France, where wings were starting to come into play (see Chapter Two). These things were little understood then and Oliver had a massive accident at Rouen from which he was lucky to escape with just cuts and bruises. 'We could not believe the wreckage,' recalled his mechanic Dave 'Beaky' Sims. Things could only get better and at Brands Hatch they did. True, neither of the factory Lotuses finished but the 49s dominated the race and at the end it was Jo Siffert who stood on the top step of the podium after winning in the Rob Walker car.

There was no stopping Matra driver Jackie Stewart in the pouring rain at the Nürburgring, although he did have one heart-stopping moment when a soon-to-be-lapped Oliver suddenly appeared in the mists ahead of him. The Scot was starting to pile on the points and was now looking a serious challenger for the World Championship. However, Hill, despite a

spin, held on through the spray to finish second and start scoring again. The rain in Germany masked the fact that the Type 49s still suffered from transmission problems, which recurred for Hill in the Oulton Park Gold Cup. While he and Oliver were racing at the Cheshire circuit, Siffert was on the continent scoring an unusual win for the Lotus 49 by scorching up the three-mile St Ursanne-Les Rangiers hillclimb in a record time.

More revisions were made to the cars to see off the Matra threat before they went to Monza, where the plan was for Hill and Oliver to be joined by a young American by the name of Mario Andretti. Chapman had been impressed by Andretti a few years earlier at Indianapolis and had promised a drive when he felt ready. It all meant extra work for the mechanics, who thought they should have been concentrating on the small matter of winning the World Championship.

Andretti was quick, even out-qualifying the local Ferraris, but perhaps that was not such a good idea. Mario's hectic weekend involved travelling to the USA on the Saturday for a road race at Indianapolis and then returning to Monza for the grand prix the following day. Somebody, perhaps Ferrari, pointed out the regulation that a driver could not compete in two such international races within 24 hours and so Andretti non-started at Monza.

None of the remaining three 49s finished the race but neither did Stewart. Hill retained the championship lead but it was tight at the top, with Ferrari's Jacky Ickx just three points behind, Stewart a further point back and McLaren driver Denny Hulme – the winner at Monza – only six points adrift of Hill. With nine points for a win and three races to go, all in North America, all four drivers were in the hunt.

The Lotus team again had a third, local driver for Canada, this time Bill Brack, who found himself on a steep learning curve. In the race Hill had to pit with broken top engine mountings but championship points were essential and he was sent on his way to secure three of them with fourth place. Reigning champion Hulme won for the second race running and now it really was tight, for he and Hill topped the table with 33 points, Stewart having finished a mere sixth following a wishbone breakage.

So to Watkins Glen and Stewart came back

with a win, but with Hulme having crashed and Hill in second place it was looking increasingly to be a battle between the two former BRM team-mates, Hill three points ahead of Stewart. There is more, though, to the story of the US Grand Prix. Andretti was back. Surprisingly, the American had never been to Watkins Glen before but he still put his car on pole. According to chief mechanic Bob Dance, Andretti told Chapman, 'You tell me when you want it on pole' – and he put it on pole. Andretti retired from the race with a clutch problem, but his time was yet to come as far as Lotus was concerned. The story continues to this day that Chapman said working with Andretti was like being with Clark again.

A pause while the 1968 Olympics took place meant that four weeks passed before the outcome of the World Championship could be decided. Despite the importance of the Mexican Grand Prix, there was again a third Lotus driver, Solana returning to the wheel of a Type 49. Chapman had also come up with an idea to make the rear wing pivot. Chapman and Bob Sparshott, Hill's mechanic, argued about the amount of fuel needed for the race. This was going to be no straightforward march to the title. To add to the tension, Siffert put the Rob Walker 49 on pole.

Siffert made a poor start, allowing Hill, who had complained that a front wheel was out of balance, to snatch the lead. By lap five Stewart had taken over at the front and when Hulme moved up to third the championship contenders occupied the front three spots. Although one of the wing-feathering bungees on Hill's rear wing had come adrift, he seemed unaffected by it and on lap nine he recaptured the lead. Shortly after, a broken damper sent Hulme's McLaren into the guardrail. One down.

Siffert, meanwhile, had been coming back into the picture. He may have been a bystander as far as the championship was concerned, but on the 22nd lap he moved into the lead, pulling away for three laps until part of the throttle linkage popped out of its socket. Thereafter Hill and Stewart remained seconds apart for lap after lap. If Stewart were to win he would take the championship, even if Hill came second, so Hill had to stay ahead. Then the fuel pressure on Stewart's Matra dropped dramatically and

he fell well back. Hill's Lotus ran faultlessly to the finish and the job was done.

After the great promise of the early season, the tragic blow of Clark's death and mid-season reliability problems, the Lotus 49 had won the World Championship, thanks in part to Hill's tenacity and determination to keep going. To add to the day's joy, Oliver came third, for only his second finish of the season. In typical Team Lotus fashion there was no time to dwell on these things for the Lotus 49s were soon off to the Tasman series again.

ABOVE **Mario Andretti: 'You tell me when you want it on pole.'** (Bob Sparshott collection)

BELOW **Graham Hill rallied the team in 1968 following Jim Clark's fatal crash.** (Bob Sparshott collection)

A time of change – or not?

Despite the success of the 1968 season, there were changes afoot at Team Lotus for 1969. For the second year running, there were different faces among the mechanics (see Chapter Four), and the driver line-up also changed. Following Clark's death, Chapman had had no choice but to throw in the young Oliver, who had experienced a difficult season. Now a particularly fast and experienced driver had become available: Jochen Rindt had yet to win a grand prix but it was obvious to many that it was just a matter of time before he did so, and the mercurial Austrian was even seen as World Championship material.

The arrival of the first non-Briton as a full-time Team Lotus driver did not amuse the 39-year-old Hill who, despite being World Champion, found himself with joint number one status. On top of this, the Lotus 49 was supposed to be on its way out, replaced by the latest thinking. The wedge-shape Type 57, with de Dion suspension front and rear, had already been abandoned as a possible replacement, but four-wheel drive was on its way. In the meantime the factory's three existing 49 chassis were overhauled and one was sold to American privateer Pete Lovely, who had tried to qualify a works Lotus 16 at Monaco back in 1959.

The season began at Kyalami with a record number of Type 49s entered. Alongside Hill and Rindt, Andretti was back for another of his occasional drives, while Siffert and John Love had their privately entered cars. They were up against a determined Stewart, eager to go one better than the previous season. Hill, running with a front wing as well as a rear one, finished an unspectacular second while Siffert was fourth.

In the non-championship Race of Champions at Brands Hatch, where Lovely joined Siffert and the works cars, Stewart finished ahead of Hill again. At a wet Silverstone International Trophy it was the spectacular Rindt's turn to finish second, on this occasion behind Jack Brabham.

The first European World Championship round of the season was held in Barcelona's Montjuich Park for the first time. It was here that the desire to fit wings of more and more ridiculous dimensions (see Chapter Two) went too far – they were a disaster waiting to happen. Early in the race, Hill's rear wing collapsed and the car crashed heavily, but Graham escaped unscathed. Observing Rindt's rear wing also lifting in the middle because of the load on the tips, he urged that his teammate be brought into the pits, but it was too late. Rindt had an almost identical accident before hitting the wreck of Hill's 49 and ending upside-down on the track, surrounded by fuel from both cars. Lotus mechanics, marshals and Hill himself extracted the Austrian with surprisingly limited injuries.

Thankfully, both drivers were relatively unharmed but one car was a write-off and the other in need of a major rebuild. The prospects for the Monaco Grand Prix, where Graham Hill was seeking his fifth victory, did not look good. Richard Attwood stood in for the not-yet-fit Rindt. In practice there was a furore over wings with the consequence that they were banned for the race; Hill's car raced instead with an engine cover tray similar to the one used the previous year.

BELOW Graham Hill escaped unscathed from the disaster at Montjuich Park in 1969, when the high-mounted rear wings collapsed on both Lotus 49s. *(Ford)*

Hill did indeed score his fifth win at Monaco in seven years and his second successive victory there with the Lotus 49. Asked immediately afterwards the secret of his Monte successes, he replied, 'It's a question of suck it and see and over the years it seems to have paid off.'

It was at this stage that Team Lotus and certain other teams started going up the blind alley that was four-wheel drive. The Type 63, though, was nowhere near ready to race and so Hill and Rindt where still in 49s when the circus reassembled at Zandvoort, over a month after Monte Carlo. Rindt, on pole, and Hill sandwiched Stewart on the front row of the grid. At the start Hill cut across his team-mate to take the lead and there was some barging between the two that probably contributed to eventual problems for both of them – the blatant rivalry between the two drivers was not helping the team. It was driveshaft failure that forced the Austrian out while leading, leaving Siffert, in one of his best performances, as the only Type 49 driver to score points, with second place.

Only 13 cars started the French Grand Prix but three of them were Team Lotus entries, John Miles débuting one of the four-wheel-drive 63s. The 49s were off the pace and

Chapman was determined that both Rindt and Hill would be in 63s for the British Grand Prix at Silverstone. To force the issue, he sold the car that Attwood had used at Monaco to the veteran Jo Bonnier. He also claimed to have sold one of the others to John Love, although the Rhodesian driver, who already had one Lotus 49, was to deny this. The Team Lotus drivers were not having any of this: they insisted on driving 49s and Chapman had to temporarily retrieve the car he had sold to Bonnier, arranging instead for the Swede to drive one of the unproven 63s alongside Miles.

This race saw Rindt come of age as a Lotus driver. It was a classic, with arguably the two best racing drivers in the world, Stewart and Rindt, battling it out, nose to tail, for many laps, the lead changing hands on more than one occasion. Hope of the win ended for the Austrian when an end plate on his rear wing came adrift and started rubbing on his left-rear tyre. He pitted for it to be ripped off by team manager Dick Scammell but such had been the domination of the two leading cars that he was able to rejoin the race without losing second place. Seven laps from the end, he ran out of fuel, and then Hill and Siffert also found

ABOVE Richard Attwood stood in for the injured Jochen Rindt at Monaco in 1969. *(Ford)*

RIGHT The Lotus 49 featured prominently on the 1969 British Grand Prix poster (right) and programme cover (far right). Despite Rindt's best efforts, the car was not to succeed that day.

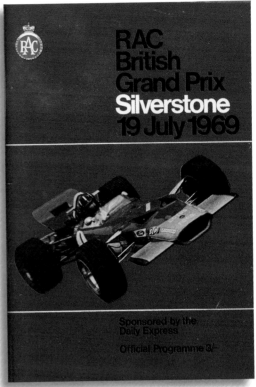

themselves short. Chapman was obsessed with putting the bare minimum of fuel in the tanks, a trait that sometimes led him into conflict with his frustrated mechanics.

Jackie Stewart was now on his way to his first World Championship and there seemed little that the Lotus 49 drivers could do about it. Reigning champion Hill's performances appeared below par while reliability was hindering Rindt's opportunities to show that he was championship material. There was no improvement in Team Lotus's fortunes at the Nürburgring, where Bonnier was able to use his 49 for the first time, qualifying slower than all but one of the Formula 2 cars that also started the race.

The Swede managed to get his car going well during practice for the non-championship Oulton Park Gold Cup, where Rindt was persuaded to race a Type 63. Then, late in practice, a bottom front wishbone came away from the upright and Bonnier's car slammed into the bank, its driver having to be taken to hospital unconscious. Bonnier was well enough the following day to attend the race as a spectator but he seemed to have lost his appetite for the Type 49 as he was not seen in one again.

Matters improved at Monza where Rindt was fastest in practice and then became part of a race-long slipstreaming battle for the lead. Into Lesmo on the last lap, he forced his way to the front only to be immediately repassed by Stewart. It was the Scot who just got to the flag first, a proverbial whisker ahead of Rindt, hotly pursued by Jean-Pierre Beltoise in a second Matra and Bruce McLaren in one of his own cars – a mere 0.19 seconds covered all four. Team Lotus, however, had now lost the championship battle: Stewart's nine points rendered the last three races of the season meaningless as far as the title was concerned.

Pete Lovely was back for the Canadian Grand Prix, where Rindt was an early leader before finishing third. It seemed a travesty that he still had not won a grand prix. However, at Watkins Glen Rindt put his 49 on pole, battled with Stewart for the lead and then raced away to victory once an oil seal had failed on his rival's Matra.

At the same time as Rindt took his first grand prix win, Hill suffered a severe accident that effectively ended his career as a top-flight driver, although he was to soldier on in Formula 1 for a number of years. Hill spun and was forced to push-start his 49, and on resuming he was unable to refasten his seat belts. A deflating tyre caused him to spin again, but this time the car overturned and Hill, unsecured in his seat, was thrown out and broke both legs.

With Hill sidelined, only three 49s – for Rindt, Siffert and Lovely – took part in the season finale in Mexico. There was a second Team Lotus entry but this was the unloved four-wheel-drive 63 that Andretti had driven in the USA and that was now entrusted to Miles again. Lovely's 49 was the only Lotus to finish, three laps behind the winner. Lotus had fallen to third place in the constructors' championship with Rindt only fourth in the drivers' table.

A last hurrah

At this point it would have been logical to write off the Type 49 as a front-line Formula 1 car. It had been designed as a simple platform for the Cosworth DFV engine, which was now widely used by Formula 1 teams in rather more sophisticated machinery, not the least of which was the dramatic, wedge-shape Lotus 72.

For the 1970 season a round of musical chairs saw Jo Siffert become a works driver with March, leaving a vacancy at Rob Walker's team. Perhaps it had become inevitable that Graham Hill's time at Team Lotus was coming to an end, for Jochen Rindt had proved to be the much quicker driver during 1969, so it was entirely appropriate that Hill should replace Siffert in the Walker team, which continued to race its Type 49. John Miles, who had persevered in testing and racing of the now-abandoned four-wheel-drive 63, stepped up to be Rindt's number two. Another driver joined the ranks of Type 49 users when Dave Charlton acquired a car, mainly for use in the South African Drivers' Championship.

A new specification of Type 49, the 49C, was introduced, as it was known that the new Type 72 would not be ready for the start of the 1970 season. Rather worryingly for Team Lotus, rival teams had their new cars ready for the start of the season.

The Lotus 49 may have been approaching obsolescence, but nevertheless there were five of them on the grid for the South African Grand Prix: the factory pair and the independent entries of a heroic Hill, still in pain from his Watkins Glen accident, John Love and Charlton. Brian Redman was on hand to drive the Rob Walker car in case Hill proved to be unfit to race. In the race Rindt collided with Jack Brabham at the first corner, but recovered ground only to retire with a blown engine. Miles, sitting in a pool of fuel, finished fifth to score his only ever points while Hill, in constant discomfort, gritted his teeth and secured a point-scoring sixth place. The best of the two locals, Charlton, had a 'what if' day, at one point running ahead of both works cars and looking as if he might finish in the points before a tyre threw its tread. His mechanics had difficulty in removing the wheel and, after they eventually did so, his DFV refused to start.

Back in Europe, Rindt, Hill and Lovely entered the Race of Champions at Brands Hatch. Practice did not go well: Rindt was fourth and a still-suffering Hill eighth, while Lovely found himself at the back of the grid, five seconds off the pole-position time. Thanks to the failures of others, Rindt finished an uneventful second, with Hill fifth.

The new Type 72s were desperately needed and made their début at the next race, the Spanish Grand Prix at Jarama. Unfortunately, it would be a difficult transition to the innovative new car, with its wedge-shape profile, side-mounted radiators, inboard brakes and radical anti-dive and anti-squat suspension design. It was the suspension in particular that proved troublesome, causing handling problems both at Jarama, where Miles even failed to qualify, and the non-championship International Trophy at Silverstone. Team Lotus still had not completely retired the Type 49 for it entered one at Jarama for local driver Alex Soler-Roig.

Perhaps not surprisingly, the 49s were then brought back into service for the Monaco Grand Prix. Here an inexperienced and understandably depressed Miles again failed to qualify. An 'upside' to this, however, was the fact that Hill, a seeded driver with an automatic place on the grid, was able to take over Miles's 49 after he had crashed the Rob Walker car and damaged its monocoque during practice. Rindt, back on the fourth row of the grid, was decidedly unhappy about the way things were looking.

Who could have predicted the thrilling way in which the race would turn out? By the end of the day, the Lotus 49 had won its last and surely most dramatic race.

Team Lotus was not happy. The 1970 International Trophy at Silverstone had shown the anti-dive, anti-squat properties of the new Lotus 72 to be a major problem. At Monaco, Jochen Rindt and John Miles were back in their elderly Type 49Cs, now fitted with the latest type of triple-blade rear aerofoil.

As usual, the entry was oversubscribed for a fixed-size grid of 16. The 10 leading drivers had a secure place but the remaining 11 had to fight it out for the other six slots. During Friday's practice it rained; Saturday was merely gloomy. Graham Hill – one of the 10 drivers with an assured place – destroyed the front end of Rob Walker's privately entered Lotus 49 going up the incline towards the Casino, putting the car out of any further participation that weekend. Suffering handling problems, Miles, however, failed to qualify and thus his car, R10, was free to be made available to the Walker team, so it was quickly repainted in Walker's dark blue livery and its cockpit was reconfigured to suit the double World Champion. There was not enough time for Hill to practise the car so he had to start from the back of the grid, from where he persevered in the race to finish fifth.

Rindt, in R6, was only eighth on the grid and it is perhaps unsurprising that the Austrian was feeling uninspired when the starter's flag fell. Circumstances allowed him to become elevated to fifth place by lap 36 and then he seemed to wake up, forcing his way past Henri Pescarolo's Matra at the Gasworks hairpin. As others ahead of him dropped out of the race, Rindt found himself in second place to Jack Brabham. The Australian, though, was extending his lead, which on lap 66 was 13.6 seconds. It seemed to be all over, with contemporary reports observing that Brabham appeared to be maintaining his lead without straining himself.

Then, for a second time in the race, Rindt is reported to have 'woken up'. With five laps to go Brabham was easing up, for he did not see Rindt as a danger. However, Colin Chapman wondered if there might be something wrong with the normally hard-charging Brabham's car, so, just in case, he urged Rindt to keep challenging.

On lap 77, with just three laps to go, Brabham was unintentionally baulked by Jo Siffert's failing March. A nine-second lead was reduced to five seconds. Rindt appeared to become inspired, sliding through Casino Square on opposite lock. By lap 78 he could see the leader. As they started the last of the 80 laps, he was only a few seconds behind. Brabham, though, was well aware of the situation and, as *Motor Sport*'s Denis Jenkinson observed, 'It all seemed to be excitement over nothing.'

The crowds were waving as, out of the Tabac corner, the Australian was just four lengths ahead. Approaching the Gasworks hairpin, he overtook Piers Courage's De Tomaso. In case Rindt should attempt to dive through on the inside of the hairpin, Brabham took a line for the apex to shut the door rather than swing out to the left as normal. Really late, he hit his tired brakes, his wheels locked and, despite trying to arrest his car with cadence braking, he glided gracefully, head-on, into the straw bales. An 'amazed and delighted' Rindt sailed past to win the race. His final lap had been achieved in 1min 23.2sec, two seconds under the previous year's fastest lap. 'Jenks' wondered if the Lotus 49 was really so obsolete, after all.

'Jochen decided that he was going to drive the wheels off the car,' recalled Team Lotus's Dick Scammell, 'and he went quicker and quicker. It was one of those days in a driver's life when he decides to hang it all out. I think that is what Jochen did and, in the end, it made the man in front make a mistake. That is why you should always keep trying in motor racing.'

BELOW Jochen Rindt's final laps in the 1970 Monaco Grand Prix were the stuff of legend. *(Ford)*

It was almost, but not quite the end, as far as the World Championship career of the Lotus 49 was concerned. Hill and Lovely continued with their private cars while Soler-Roig failed to qualify a factory 49 for the French Grand Prix at Clermont-Ferrand. The Lotus 72 was now becoming a regular race winner and Rindt was looking the increasingly likely winner of the World Championship.

The last, but significant, entries for a works 49 were in Britain, Germany and Austria. The very promising young Brazilian, Emerson Fittipaldi, had put off Chapman's offer of a Formula 1 drive until he thought he was ready. Making his début in the British Grand Prix at Brands Hatch, Fittipaldi indicated maturity with a sensible drive to eighth place. The Lotus 49, however, was really showing its age by now: the three of them in this race – driven by Fittipaldi, Hill and Lovely – occupied the back row of the grid.

It was at the next race, the German Grand Prix at Hockenheim, that Fittipaldi really showed promise of what was to come, emerging from a midfield battle in a fine fourth place in the 49. After that race, Rob Walker decided that his 49 was no longer up to it and sat back to wait for a Type 72 of his own. The final World Championship race for a Type 49 came in Austria at the Österreichring, where Fittipaldi had problems with his car's fuel mixture. Lovely entered his 49 for the US Grand Prix but failed to qualify.

At Monza Rindt was tragically killed in his Lotus 72 during practice for the Italian Grand Prix. The World Championship nevertheless went posthumously to Rindt for his nearest challenger, Ferrari's Jacky Ickx, was unable to score enough points during the remaining three rounds to overtake the Austrian's score. It may seem of little importance given the circumstances, but the Lotus 49 – thanks to that victory in Monte Carlo – had played its part in winning another World Championship for Team Lotus.

As far as works cars were concerned, the story had almost ended for the Lotus 49. There were just two appearances in 1971, both in non-championship races, allowing Wilson Fittipaldi (Emerson's older brother) and Tony Trimmer to experience the car.

Thereafter, Lotus 49s only raced in anger in South Africa. In August 1972 Meyer Botha, in R8, the car that Dave Charlton had originally taken to the region, had a massive accident during a South African Drivers' Championship race. Botha escaped relatively unscathed but the car was heavily damaged. The Lotus 49's history as a contemporary racing car was over, five years after it had made its mark on motor racing history.

The DFV continues

The Cosworth DFV, the engine that the 49 had been built to carry, still had plenty of life left in it. Indeed, it would power Lotus to two more World Championship titles. Coincidentally, both of these winners, Emerson Fittipaldi (Type 72, 1972) and Mario Andretti (Type 79, 1978) had started their grand prix careers at the wheel of Lotus 49s. Other DFV drivers to take the championship were Jackie Stewart, James Hunt, Alan Jones, Nelson Piquet and Keke Rosberg, the last in 1982. By that stage the DFV had become unquestionably the most successful grand prix power unit of all time.

Lotus last used the DFV in 1983, the final time being when Nigel Mansell retired his Type 92 in Canada. There were more wins to come for Lotus, but not many. With Renault and then Honda engines, Team Lotus scored six more victories before the team effectively closed down at the end of 1994. Compare that to the 45 grand prix wins that Team Lotus achieved with the Cosworth DFV, 11 of them with the Type 49.

BELOW The Cosworth DFV continued to power Lotus to victory long after the 49 had been retired, most notably with the Type 72. (Author)

ABOVE The Tasman series was the only time Jim Clark was seen in a Lotus 49 in Gold Leaf livery. *(Ford)*

THE TASMAN SERIES

Twice factory Lotus 49s went 'down under' for the Tasman series. With the management many thousands of miles away, it was almost a holiday for the team. The Tasman was a championship of two halves, one in New Zealand and the other in Australia, and ran from 1964 to 1975. In its earlier years it attracted a good number of British Formula 1 teams and drivers.

The original formula was set at 2½ litres, initially to make use of obsolete F1 engines from the pre-1961 period. In later years, after Lotus had quit the Tasman scene, Formula 5000 cars were brought in. Team Lotus joined the show in 1965 and Jim Clark used the one-off Type 32B, a Formula 2 car converted to run with a four-cylinder 2½-litre Coventry Climax FPF engine, to take the title first time out. BRM then proved that the way to go was to install a stretched version of the V8 that had been used in the 1961–65 period, the 1½-litre

years of Formula 1. Lotus got the message after Clark won just one round in 1966 and returned with a 1.9-litre Climax version of its Type 33 F1 car. The Scotsman accordingly took his second Tasman Cup.

Rather than continue to use a stretched engine from Formula 1's 1½-litre era, Lotus now turned to a shrunken 2½-litre short-stroke version of the Cosworth DFV. This was fitted to two Lotus 49s (R1 and R2) converted to what was called 49T specification and entered for Clark and Hill, although the latter only drove in Australia. The DFW, as the 2½-litre engine was known, was peaky and Keith Duckworth admitted that reducing the DFV by 500cc cost more than he had imagined in terms of power. Nevertheless, Clark saw off a challenge from Ferrari's Chris Amon to win what would be his last title. With the arrival of the Gold Leaf colour scheme and the rear wing experiment (see pages 26 and 27), the 1968 Tasman series had been memorable for Team Lotus for more than one reason. Clark's victory in the 1968 Australian Grand Prix, his fourth in the series that year, would be his last before his fatal accident.

The following year, 1969, Hill and Rindt were sent 'down under' with a pair of 2½-litre 49Bs, R8 and R9, but Amon now had the upper hand in his Ferrari. Rindt out-qualified his team-mate first time out on his début in a Type 49 and in fact he proved to be consistently quicker than Hill, causing relationships to become strained. Cosworth reliability became a problem and Mike Costin himself flew out to resolve this. Then when Rindt crashed at Levin there were not enough parts on hand to repair the car so the original Type 49B, R5, which was yet to be updated to 1969 specification, was sent out for duty within 12 hours of news of the mishap reaching Hethel. Rindt won the next race and then repeated Clark's victory of the year before in the Warwick Farm 100, but these two successes were not enough. Despite the fact that Team Lotus had started as favourite, the 1969 Tasman title fell to Ferrari and Lotus left the series, never to return.

ABOVE Everybody helped out on the Tasman series. This is Jim Clark in New Zealand during 1968. *(Ferret Fotographics)*

BELOW LEFT The Tasman series was a time for play for the European drivers, including Jim Clark. *(Ford)*

BELOW A wing was briefly fixed to a Lotus 49 for the first time during the 1968 Tasman series. The next time the cars returned 'down under' they were all the rage. *(Ferret Fotographics)*

Lotus 49 drivers

Between 1967 and 1972, a total of 23 drivers raced Lotus 49s. Of these, 15 drove for the factory, although some were only one-offs.

In total 16 drivers competed in World Championship grands prix in Lotus 49s. A further two practised but did not start, while five only drove such a car in non-championship races.

Four drivers – Jim Clark, Graham Hill, Jochen Rindt and Jo Siffert – won grands prix in Lotus 49s.

Jim Clark

Five GP wins with Lotus 49 (25 GP wins overall, World Champion with Lotus-Climax 25 in 1963 and Lotus-Climax 33 in 1965); Tasman Champion 1968 with Lotus 49

Scotsman Jim Clark has to be one of the candidates for the 'greatest ever' racing driver. Forever associated with Lotus – he had a close rapport with Colin Chapman – there were times during the 1½-litre era when he totally dominated the scene. The Lotus mechanics also recalled how gentle he was with cars. 'Jimmy would use less petrol, less brakes and go slightly faster,' Jim Endruweit once recalled. He was tremendously versatile, winning the

Indianapolis 500 in 1965 and being a joy to watch at the wheel of a Lotus Cortina.

It was Clark who scored the fairy-tale victory for the Lotus 49 on its début in Holland, the first of four wins that year. However, mechanical unreliability mid-season meant that he was unable to take the World Championship that year. He did, though, give the Lotus 49 its first championship title when he took his third Tasman Cup early in 1968. Having won the World Championship in 1963 and '65, a third crown seemed to be beckoning in 1968, but Clark was tragically killed in a Formula 2 race at Hockenheim. He won five of the 10 races that he started with the Lotus 49.

'Jimmy, God bless him, was a gentleman and easy to work for,' said his former mechanic Dick Scammell. 'He knew what he wanted and inspired you to do a good job. You knew that if you gave him the car he would deliver. Jimmy would drive with all sorts of things hanging off and make up for the inadequacies of the vehicle.'

During 1967 Clark and Graham Hill theoretically had joint number one status at Lotus but, recalled mechanic Bob Dance, 'we knew that one was more number one than the other'.

'It gave me real pride that he trusted me to look after his car and I worked very hard not to lose that trust,' said Allan McCall, who looked after Clark's Type 49 in 1967.

'Very easy-going and introverted,' was how his former girlfriend Sally Stokes (now Swart) described him.

Graham Hill

World Champion 1968 with Lotus 49; four GP wins with Lotus 49 (14 GP wins overall, also World Champion in 1962 with BRM)

It is often said that whereas Clark was a natural, the tenacious Graham Hill had to work hard at achieving his results. 'He was definitely determined,' said Bob Sparshott, Hill's mechanic during the 1968 championship-winning year. Hill did not enjoy quite the same close relationship with Chapman as Clark did, having been used to making the decisions himself at BRM.

After Clark's death, Hill produced plenty

BELOW Clark and Chapman enjoy victory after the 1968 South African Grand Prix. *(Ford)*

of that determination to win the World Championship in a Lotus 49. It was his second title, his first having come in 1962 with a 1½-litre BRM, although he had started his Formula 1 career with Lotus. A master at Monte Carlo, he is the only driver ever to have won the World Championship, Le Mans 24 Hours and the Indianapolis 500. While Clark took the lion's share of the glory in 1967, it must not be forgotten that Hill did much of the initial testing and was responsible for much of the development of the 49 and the Cosworth DFV engine.

Although never the same driver after the injuries he suffered at Watkins Glen in 1969, Hill went on to race for Rob Walker (in both Lotus 49 and 72) and Brabham before forming his own team. He died when trying to land his aircraft in fog in 1975.

'Graham was a lovely lad, hugely entertaining

LEFT **Graham Hill with Ford's Harley Copp.**
(Ford)

but he was so pernickety,' recalls Dick Scammell. 'He had his own notebook and he wrote everything down in it, every setting – you name it, he had it down. We would go round and round in circles and then probably end up using the settings that were on the other car. Graham was very demanding but a wonderful character.'

Bob Sparshott: 'Graham could be very awkward but we used to have some fun with him. He knew that he gave us aggro and so might reward us afterwards. He would end up being one of the boys.'

Jochen Rindt
World Champion in 1970 with Lotus 49 and Lotus 72; two GP wins with Lotus 49 (six GP wins overall)

At the 1970 Monaco Grand Prix the mercurial Austrian scored what was arguably the Lotus 49's finest win.

Jochen Rindt had first come to prominence when he took on the established stars in Formula 2. As a result he had a one-off drive for Rob Walker before joining Cooper in 1965. Three years with the Cooper team, by now in decline, and a further season with Brabham brought no success and it was in search of victory that he reluctantly joined Team Lotus for 1969, becoming its first non-British regular driver. Chapman was to find him the most 'complicated' driver he had worked with.

The elusive first grand prix win came at the end of 1969 in the US Grand Prix. The following season, using the 49 and the new 72, Rindt was the class of the field, taking five wins in all. He was killed at the Italian Grand Prix when his car swerved into the crash barrier. In the subsequent races his nearest rival, Jacky Ickx, was unable to score enough points to overtake him and Rindt therefore became Formula 1's only posthumous World Champion.

Rindt was also one of four Lotus 49 drivers – along with Jackie Oliver, Richard Attwood and Graham Hill – to win the Le Mans 24 Hours.

RIGHT Jochen Rindt at Silverstone in 1969. *(Ford)*

Jo Siffert
One GP win with Lotus 49 (two GP wins overall)

The last person to win a World Championship race with an independently entered car, Swiss driver Jo Siffert first entered grand prix racing with Ecurie Filipinetti's Lotus 24 and then his own. Sometimes underrated, 'Seppe' joined Rob Walker in 1962, moving on to March and then BRM. It was with the latter that he scored his second grand prix win, the 1971 Austrian race at the Österreichring. He was killed in the final Formula 1 race of that year, a non-championship event at Brands Hatch.

Siffert was one of the fastest drivers of his day but there were times when his valour was the better part of his discretion. He was also a very fine sports car driver and one of the stars of John Wyer's Gulf-backed Porsche 917 team.

Other Lotus 49 drivers
Team Lotus used two other regular 'number two' drivers, both Englishmen, during the Lotus 49 era: Jackie Oliver, who was thrown in at the proverbial deep end in 1968 after Jim Clark's death, and John Miles, who had brief acquaintance with the car in 1970 before its successor, the Type 72, was ready to race.

Oliver was at Team Lotus for just the one season, and later raced in Formula 1 for BRM, McLaren and Shadow, but with little success. The highlight of his Formula 1 career came when he led the British Grand Prix in his 49. Although he regarded himself as a single-seater man, his best results came in sports cars, and he won Le Mans in 1969 and the Can-Am title in 1974. He went on to be one of the directors of the Arrows Formula 1 team.

Miles, by contrast, only ever raced in Formula 1 for Team Lotus, leaving the team, disillusioned, following Rindt's fatal crash. It was an inappropriate end to the grand prix career of a man who was described by *Autocourse*, after the 1969 season, as 'the discovery of the year as far as Formula 1 is concerned'.

During this period Team Lotus would often engage a paying driver, usually a local man, to drive a third factory car. Mexican Moises Solana benefited the most from this, racing a Type 49 in three grands prix. Others to drive under this policy were Italian Giancarlo Baghetti (who in 1961, driving for Ferrari, won on his grand prix début only for his career later to nosedive), Spaniard Alex Soler-

ABOVE Moises Solana's Lotus 49 ahead of Denny Hulme's Brabham in the 1967 Mexican Grand Prix. *(sutton-images.com)*

RIGHT Eppie Wietzes was the first of two Canadians who drove the Lotus 49. *(sutton-images.com)*

Roig (who twice failed to qualify for a World Championship grand prix with a 49) and Canadians Eppie Wietzes and Bill Brack, the latter the Lotus importer who later recalled paying $6,000 for his drive.

Of more significance were the other names who, for a variety of reasons, had occasional drives in a Lotus 49. Two future World Champions, Mario Andretti and Emerson Fittipaldi, made their grand prix débuts in 49s, both of them impressing first time out. The 1970 Le Mans winner, Richard Attwood, also had a one-off drive with a 49, replacing an injured Rindt for the 1969 Monaco Grand Prix. In addition to all the above, Emerson's brother Wilson and Tony Trimmer both drove a Team Lotus 49 in non-championship races.

Recalling the two future World Champions, Dick Scammell said, 'Mario was a real professional. Some drivers used to go home and come back in the morning but others, like Mario, would like to hang around and discuss things with the mechanics, which

helped. I remember we took Emerson and some others for a test drive. The thing about Emerson was that he was quick and looked as if he would have an accident at any moment... but he didn't. He was so enthusiastic, good to work with.'

Other contemporary 49 drivers who competed in grands prix, albeit in privately entered cars, were Jo Bonnier, Pete Lovely, John Love and Dave Charlton. Peter Parnell, Peter de Klerk and Meyer Botha also drove 49s but only in the South African Drivers' Championship.

Finally, Brian Redman was on hand to drive the Rob Walker car in practice for the 1970 South African Grand Prix in case Graham Hill was not sufficiently fit following his Watkins Glen accident the year before. In 1968, on the morning of the Belgian Grand Prix, Redman had agreed to join Lotus once his Cooper contract had expired, but an accident in that race effectively ended his grand prix career and the Lotus drive never happened.

The designers

Colin Chapman

Colin Chapman was one of the most significant figures in motor racing during the second half of the 20th century. He took his marque, Lotus, from a one-man band (with help from wife Hazel) building a trials special to a position as one of the leading manufacturers in motor racing, winning seven constructors' World Championships, six drivers' titles and 73 grands prix. In addition, Lotus became the first British constructor to win the Indianapolis 500.

Under Chapman's guidance, Lotus Cars became a manufacturer of charismatic road-going sports cars. Asked whether the racing assisted the development of the road cars, Chapman replied, 'I go racing because I like it but I do like the technical fall-out that comes from it.'

A qualified structural engineer, Chapman was still working for British Aluminium when he built up his first car. Within six years, Lotus cars were being entered for grands prix, Cliff Allison

ABOVE Bill Brack drove a Lotus 49 in the 1969 Canadian Grand Prix.

(sutton-images.com)

RIGHT Colin Chapman was more than capable of driving one of his own Lotus 49s. *(Ford)*

finishing fourth in the Belgian Grand Prix. Already a builder of sports racing cars, Team Lotus became a leading supplier of single-seaters in a whole variety of formulae. The first grand prix win came when Stirling Moss took the 1960 Monaco Grand Prix in Rob Walker's Lotus 18. by introducing monocoque design to Formula 1 in 1962 with the Lotus 25, Chapman rendered the competition obsolete. Jim Clark, a driver with whom Chapman had a close rapport, delivered Team Lotus's first World Championship in 1963.

A forthright yet inspiring man who worked his employees hard, Chapman was one of the few to whom the description 'genius' really could be applied. He did not always get it right but when he did motor racing moved up another notch. His early days driving his own cars indicated that he was also a talented driver. Having been instrumental in the redesign of the Vanwall, he was offered a drive by Tony Vandervell in the 1956 French Grand Prix but failed to start following a practice accident.

As Dick Scammell recalls, 'Colin was very good at handling people. I used to get really uptight and say, "that's it", but then change my mind. He could easily sum you up.'

Bob Dance, another chief mechanic on the 49, added that 'he was able to charm' while also observing that 'the old man would incite panic'. Dance recalled one of the drivers that Chapman respected the most, Mario Andretti, giving advice to his boss: 'Colin, calm down. When you panic, they all panic.'

Maurice Phillippe

Chapman may have been responsible for the overall design of the Lotus 49 but much of the detail work was carried out by designer/draughtsman Maurice Phillippe. The pair are said to have had many of their discussions regarding design of the car when they were travelling, whether to meetings with Cosworth or ZF, or to races.

RIGHT Chapman keeps an eye on the progress of the Type 49s at the 1967 British Grand Prix. *(Ford)*

The intuitive and fast-working Phillippe, a former aerospace designer and Ford development engineer, joined Team Lotus on the recommendation of his predecessor Len Terry. Like Terry and Chapman, he had been involved in the 750 formula. His initial task was to draw the BRM H16-engined Type 43 for 1966. In preparation for 1967 he worked on the Type 49, of course, as well as new Lotus Cortinas and alternatives for the Indianapolis car.

His colleague, Martin Waide, recalled, 'In its early stages the 49 had quite a few problems and it was a testing time for Maurice; I think he sorely tried Chapman's patience.' Nevertheless, Scammell said, 'Maurice was great to work with – he and Colin seemed to understand each other.'

Mechanic Dave Sims recalled how Phillippe, if he needed to explain the geometry of the car, would roll up his sleeves and show the mechanics: 'He did that quite a bit – he was a practical guy.'

Phillippe worked with Chapman on the subsequent Lotus Formula 1 winner, the Type 72, an innovative design that took the Cosworth DFV a step further towards immortality. Waide believes that Phillippe's work was more in the nature of 'artistic renderings'. This tended to result in attractive-looking cars with parts that could sometimes fail.

Phillippe went on to design both Indianapolis and Formula 1 cars for Vel's Parnelli Racing, which he joined in 1971. From there he became chief designer for Tyrrell before setting up his own consultancy. He died in 1989.

Keith Duckworth

A mechanical engineering student at Imperial College, Keith Duckworth was an early Lotus customer, having bought a Type 6 kit car to go racing in 1953. A few races showed him that he was not cut out to be a racing driver but he started working at the company during his vacations. In 1957 Chapman offered him a full-time position as a gearbox development engineer. His future business partner Mike Costin also joined Team Lotus in the mid-1950s as technical director.

Duckworth had not been at Lotus for long when he disagreed with Chapman over the development of an unreliable five-speed sequential gearbox nicknamed the 'Queerbox'. In September 1958, he and Costin formed a new company to offer design and development services to motor sport. Costin, though, had just signed a three-year contract with Lotus and so Cosworth, as the new company was called, operated initially as a one-man band.

Cosworth grew quickly, particularly once Duckworth began work on Ford 105E-based engines for Formula Junior. The Formula 3 MAE, another modified Anglia power unit, and the Formula 2 SCA both led the field in their respective formulae. New regulations for Formula 2 in 1967 saw the introduction of the equally successful FVA. It was perhaps logical that in seeking someone to build an engine for the new 3-litre Formula 1, Chapman should turn to his former employee, despite the fact that Duckworth had never designed a complete engine from scratch. All was made possible thanks to Ford money and the faith shown by its director of public affairs, Walter Hayes, in Duckworth. By the end of the 1967 season Duckworth was being described in the press as 'the world's leading engine designer'.

Duckworth's DFV went on to be the most successful grand prix engine of all time, winning 155 Formula 1 races – 47 of them with Team Lotus – between 1967 and 1985. Variants of the engine were used in sportscar and Indycar racing, twice winning at Le Mans and ten times in the Indianapolis 500.

The direct but inspirational Duckworth sold his majority stake in Cosworth in 1980 but remained as chairman for seven years until major heart surgery meant that he had to relinquish this post. He was made honorary life president in 1989 and died in 2005.

BELOW Keith Duckworth and Maurice Phillippe oversee an early Lotus 49 test. *(Ford)*

'Formula for success.'

James Tosen
Autocar

Chapter Two

Anatomy of the Lotus 49

The Lotus 49 was designed as a straightforward monocoque racing car built to carry the new Cosworth DFV engine. Initially unreliable but with a structural integrity that rebuffed Colin Chapman's critics, it was developed into a World Championship winner, its original clean lines transformed by the advent of aerodynamic aids.

OPPOSITE An early-specification Lotus 49 – this is R3 – with nose cone removed to reveal water radiator, oil tank, front bulkhead and front suspension. *(Author)*

ABOVE Earliest example of the Type 49 at Hethel: Maurice Phillippe and Colin Chapman look on as Graham Hill examines his new mount for 1967. Hazel and a young Clive Chapman appear unimpressed. *(Ford)*

ABOVE Hill flies a Type 49B at the Nürburgring in 1969. *(Ford)*

BELOW Type 49C specification was brought in for 1970: Hill's Rob Walker 49C leads John Surtees (Surtees), Dan Gurney (McLaren) and Chris Amon (March) at Brands Hatch. *(Ford)*

BELOW The 'T' in Type 49T stands for Tasman – this is Hill in 1968. *(Ford)*

LOTUS 49 KEY FACTS

There were four evolutionary stages in the life of the Lotus 49, as follows:

Lotus 49

The original specification for the car with ZF 5DS12 gearbox, used during 1967.

Lotus 49B

The cars were comprehensively reworked early in 1968 to provide greater rearward weight bias and to use a Hewland gearbox. Overall weight increased by 78lb to 1,180lb 'dry' and 1,640lb 'ready to race'.

Lotus 49C

Four chassis – R6, R7, R8 and R10 – were redesignated 49C following the fitting of new 13in front wheels and tyres and consequent modifications to the front suspension.

Lotus 49T

Team Lotus entered the 1968 and 1969 Tasman series in New Zealand and Australia. To conform to the engine capacity limit, the cars were fitted with a 2½-litre version of the Cosworth DFV, designated the DFW. Thus powered, the cars were known as 49Ts. The cars for the 1969 series were really hybrids, original-specification 49s with 49B-style lower radius rod mountings and a high wing.

Writing in *Autocar* during July 1967, James Tosen stated: 'Seldom has a car so substantiated the dictum that if it looks right it is right.' The design of the Lotus 49 was straightforward, with nothing particularly innovative, although the integrated nature of the car and its Cosworth DFV engine set a trend.

As historian Doug Nye observed, Colin Chapman's touch was evident in the detail, for there was just enough car to do the job of carrying Ford's new Cosworth DFV. The engine was untried and it was considered important for the chassis to be simple and trouble-free – the relatively complex Lotus 72 was yet to come. If truth be told, the Type 49 should have been something of a short-term expediency, but the failure of the Lotus 63 four-wheel-drive car during 1969 meant that the old model remained Team Lotus's front-line weapon for three full seasons, and for part of a fourth season when it still proved to be a winner.

Lotus historian Michael Oliver has pointed out that the Type 49 was Chapman's first Formula 1 car in which he was not constrained by having to design around an existing engine. As far as Chapman was concerned, there was to be only one unknown quality about the car, and that was to be the power unit.

Chassis

The Lotus 49 was based on a simple, twin-boom, true monocoque fuselage. In this respect it was similar in style to its immediate predecessor, the BRM H16-engined Lotus 43 that won the 1966 US Grand Prix. However, the size of the Cosworth DFV engine meant that the chassis was scaled down in comparison.

The fully stressed and 'naked' engine rested close to the rear of the monocoque. Starting at

BELOW An early drawing from August 1966 shows the proposed radiator installation for the new Formula 1 car. *(Classic Team Lotus)*

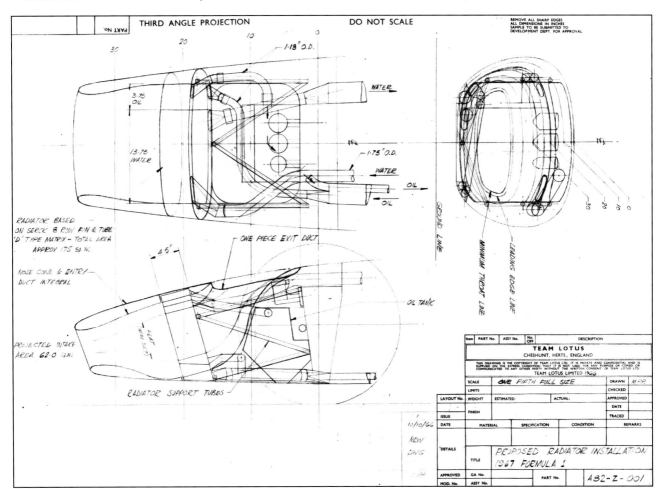

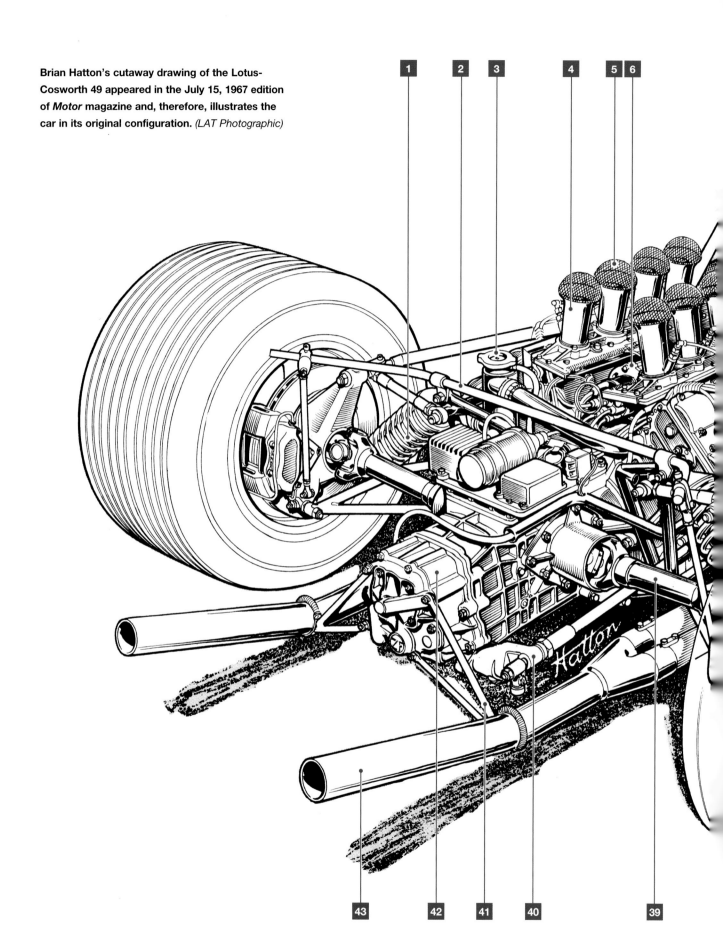

Brian Hatton's cutaway drawing of the Lotus-Cosworth 49 appeared in the July 15, 1967 edition of *Motor* magazine and, therefore, illustrates the car in its original configuration. *(LAT Photographic)*

1 2 3 4 5 6

43 42 41 40 39

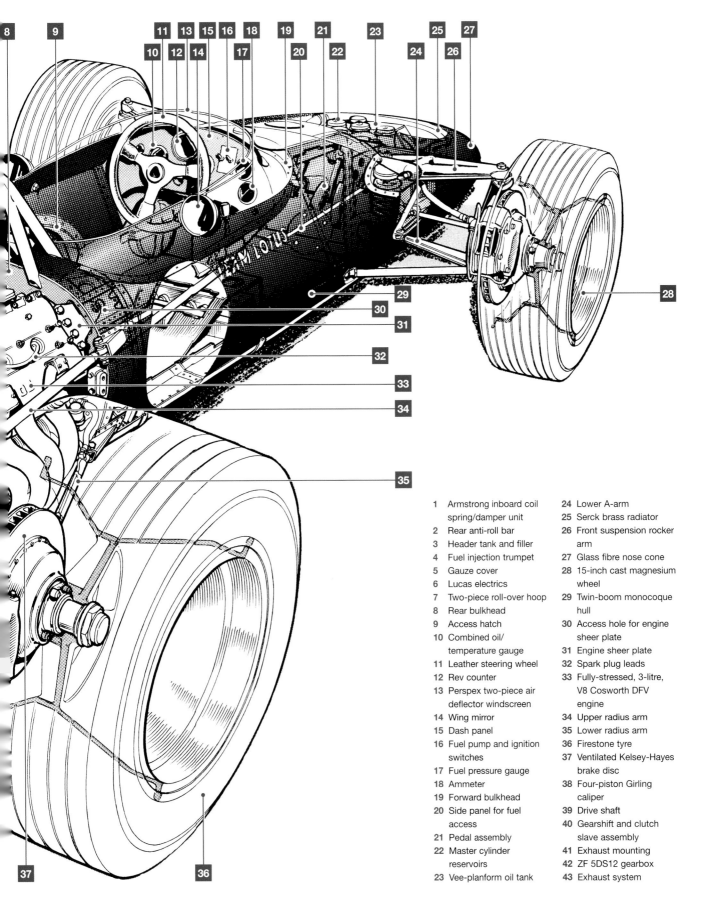

1 Armstrong inboard coil
   spring/damper unit
2 Rear anti-roll bar
3 Header tank and filler
4 Fuel injection trumpet
5 Gauze cover
6 Lucas electrics
7 Two-piece roll-over hoop
8 Rear bulkhead
9 Access hatch
10 Combined oil/
   temperature gauge
11 Leather steering wheel
12 Rev counter
13 Perspex two-piece air
   deflector windscreen
14 Wing mirror
15 Dash panel
16 Fuel pump and ignition
   switches
17 Fuel pressure gauge
18 Ammeter
19 Forward bulkhead
20 Side panel for fuel
   access
21 Pedal assembly
22 Master cylinder
   reservoirs
23 Vee-planform oil tank

24 Lower A-arm
25 Serck brass radiator
26 Front suspension rocker
   arm
27 Glass fibre nose cone
28 15-inch cast magnesium
   wheel
29 Twin-boom monocoque
   hull
30 Access hole for engine
   sheer plate
31 Engine sheer plate
32 Spark plug leads
33 Fully-stressed, 3-litre,
   V8 Cosworth DFV
   engine
34 Upper radius arm
35 Lower radius arm
36 Firestone tyre
37 Ventilated Kelsey-Hayes
   brake disc
38 Four-piston Girling
   caliper
39 Drive shaft
40 Gearshift and clutch
   slave assembly
41 Exhaust mounting
42 ZF 5DS12 gearbox
43 Exhaust system

47

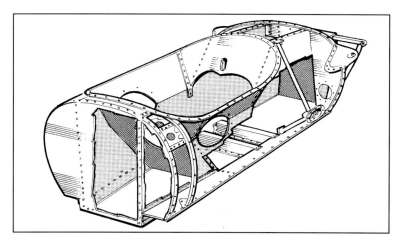

LEFT The monocoque hull was more cylindrical than those of previous Lotuses, with the inside folded from one sheet, belled out and filleted to form the cockpit, as seen in this 1967 Brian Hatton drawing. *(LAT Photographic)*

BELOW LEFT The H16-engined Type 43 was the first Lotus to have its engine bolted to the back of the hull. *(Andy Brown)*

BELOW The water pipe was positioned outside the monocoque on the left-hand side. *(Author)*

BELOW This view of the radiator on R3 also shows the original oil tank, which was vee-shaped to deflect the air out through the front suspension. *(Author)*

the rear mounting point for the front suspension rocker arms and ending behind the driver's back, the monocoque was skinned in L72 Alclad aluminium alloy shaped over and riveted to internal mild-steel bulkheads; the monocoques of R1 and R2 were made from 18swg sheet, whereas subsequent cars used heavier 16swg sheet. The underside of the monocoque was

stepped to form channels on both sides for oil and water pipes. A large-diameter water pipe was mounted externally, midway on the left-hand side of the monocoque.

There were full 360° stressed sections in the scuttle and behind the cockpit. A rectangular footbox was built around suspension-supporting square tube frames and riveted to the front of the tub. Ahead of the footbox, which contained the steering rack, was a vee-planform oil tank, which was simply attached by a rubber bungee. The triangular shape was chosen to help channel air sideways as it exited the front-mounted radiator.

A light tubular subframe supported a Serck brass radiator with twin cores, one for water, one for oil. This subframe also acted as the forward mounting point for the suspension's cast-alloy rocker arms, while the rearward mounting point protruded outwards from the front of the monocoque within a stubby fairing.

The driver's seat back formed the 10-gallon centre tank's forward-sloping bulkhead, the monocoque terminating, flat-faced, in the tank's rear closing plate. After the 1967 British Grand Prix, an aluminium-sheet bulkhead was added to R1 to give greater torsional integrity to the front of the monocoque; after the Italian Grand Prix R2 was similarly modified and this feature was incorporated on all further chassis. However, while R1 now featured an oval access hatch combined with the fuel filler, the filler cap on R2 uniquely remained separate from a larger access hatch.

Within the cockpit the inner faces of the side booms carried access hatches to the internal tank space and also helped to give the drivers necessary elbow room. Two FPT rubber fuel bags, each with a capacity of 15 gallons, were inserted through these access hatches (one bag on each side), 'wrestled' into position and piped up.

The side tanks drained through non-return valves into the centre tank. Fuel pick-up was in the base of the centre tank via a pot that was topped up with fuel from the side cells as the car accelerated, the fuel passing through one-way valves into the centre tank.

The pedal assembly on the first two chassis was reached for service and adjustment by means of a small, circular access plate on the top of the scuttle. In practice this aperture proved to be too small, so all subsequent chassis were provided with a much larger rectangular hatch. To compensate for this larger cut-out, on these later cars the torsion boxes in this area were also strengthened by means of two extra internal bulkheads, which required the main pontoon bag tanks to be slightly shortened.

The glass-fibre nose cone was the only detachable body panel. The first time Lotus had used a detachable nose had been on the previous year's BRM H16-engined Type 43. A Lotus 49 appeared with a different nose on just one occasion – the 1967 British Grand Prix – because there was no spare glass-fibre nose available following Graham Hill's practice

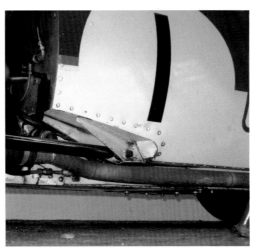

ABOVE The double roll-over hoop. *(Author)*

ABOVE RIGHT The rear stays for the 49C roll-over hoop were mounted on the engine. *(Author)*

crash; on this occasion use was made of an early aluminium buck that made the car look more like a Type 33 from the front, although the respective designs of the two cars meant that there was no way that this nose could have come from a 33. An earlier style of air deflector was also fitted to Hill's car for this one race.

At the rear, triangulated tubular frames provided inboard pick-ups on the cylinder heads, with a cross beam offering lower mounts bolted

beneath the gearbox. A two-piece roll-over hoop was located just behind the driver's head.

During early 1968, new, wider tyres (see 'Wheels and tyres') meant that the 49s became more prone to slipping and sliding at the rear. One of the ways in which this was overcome was evaluated on R5 at the Race of Champions at Brands Hatch: more weight was placed at the rear by the use of a large oil tank fitted saddle-style over the gearbox and carrying a

RIGHT Fuel tank access located in the seat back. *(Author)*

FAR RIGHT The oil tank was moved from the nose for weight distribution, becoming a saddle tank over the gearbox, which was now of Hewland manufacture. *(Author)*

RIGHT The mount for the top radius arm; note the access hole for the engine sheer plate. *(Author)*

FAR RIGHT The water header tank and filler cap. *(Author)*

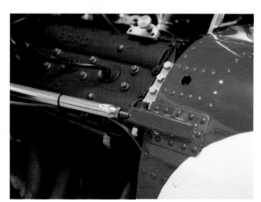

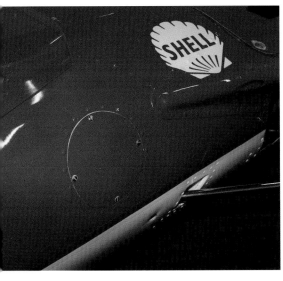

small oil cooler on the top, thereby relieving the nose radiator of its oil-cooling function.

Hot air from the nose-mounted radiators caused excess heat in the cockpit. An attempt to overcome this, and to improve aerodynamic performance, was eventually made by fitting top-ducted radiators with lipped and ramped vents in the top of the nose cone to funnel expended radiator air upwards. Although this modification improved matters, it was never a complete solution.

New regulations introduced by the FIA for the 1969 season included the requirement to fit a full fire extinguisher system and a more substantial roll-over hoop, so the existing 49s were modified to suit.

Aerodynamics

During 1968 Lotus raced its first wedge-shape car, the Type 56, which led the Indianapolis 500. As the Lotus 49 featured a traditional front-mounted radiator, it was never likely to match the aerodynamic efficiency possible with a wedge profile.

Other than its uncovered power unit, there was little in terms of shape to distinguish the Lotus 49 from the Coopers that had started the rear-engined revolution in Formula 1 in the late 1950s. However, with the introduction of the 49B in 1968, moves were made to create an outline as near to that of a wedge as possible while still retaining a nose-mounted radiator. The clean and basic look of the Lotus 49 became a thing of the past.

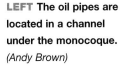

ABOVE LEFT Side panel for fuel access. *(Author)*

ABOVE The original position of the fuel pump before the lower radius arm was relocated. *(Andy Brown)*

LEFT The oil pipes are located in a channel under the monocoque. *(Andy Brown)*

LEFT Top of monocoque detail on R10. *(Author)*

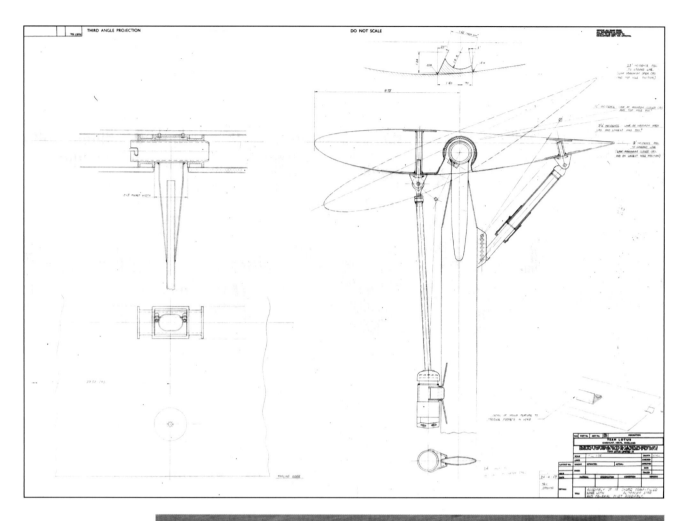

ABOVE Foam-filled wing with aluminium spar and co-axial pivot assembly as drawn in April 1969. *(Classic Team Lotus)*

RIGHT Hill's car at Monaco in 1968 featured a cuneiform engine and gearbox cowl with a NACA duct that fed an oil cooler matrix. *(Ford)*

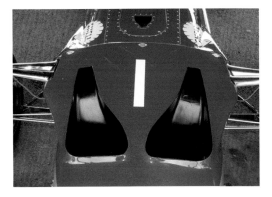

The nose cone was largely unchanged, apart from having a pair of aerofoil-section fins. However, the naked DFV – a feature of the car during its first season – was now partially covered by a cuneiform glass-fibre engine and gearbox cowl. This incorporated a deck-top NACA duct that fed an oil cooler matrix buried beneath. Expended air exited through a vent in the cowl's rear transom. The result of these changes was that the total download force now acted about the 49's centre of gravity. The car ran in this configuration for just three races.

During practice for the 1967 Belgian Grand Prix, the Lotus 49s had appeared with bib spoilers. Although effective in countering negative lift at high speed, they made the back end unstable and were removed for the race. Drawings were also produced that year of an 'aerofoil assembly', a fin attached to either side of the nose but higher than the big spoiler, but this idea was not adopted.

Two ducted air exits were cut in the top of the nose prior to the 1968 Italian Grand Prix and these replaced the exits on either side of the nose that had been used previously. They provided significant additional downforce and meant that the front nose fins could be reduced in size.

The 1968 season also saw wings start to sprout on Formula 1 cars – a trend that overtook Team Lotus's idea of the semi-wedge. There was nothing new in the concept, as history records several earlier avenues of similar thinking. At the Nürburgring in 1956 young Swiss driver Michael May fitted a large, cumbersome wing to his production Porsche 550 Spyder only for it to be banned after the car set a very competitive practice time thanks to its increased grip. About a decade later Jim Hall revived the idea for his Chaparral

2E. McLaren experimented with a wing on its prototype single-seater in 1966 but, despite the fact that it knocked whole seconds off a lap time, the idea was shelved – its young designer Robin Herd still wonders why.

So it was that Ferrari and Brabham were the first in Formula 1 to use the idea when their cars appeared at the 1968 Belgian Grand Prix with strutted, chassis-mounted rear aerofoils and nose-mounted trim vanes. By the next race, Team Lotus had followed suit. This would indicate an instance of Lotus being a follower, but that would be a little unfair on the young mechanics who had run the Lotus 49 in similar guise during the Tasman series the previous winter.

During that Tasman campaign the first appearance of a wing on a Lotus 49 (R2) was

a brief one, resulting from Jim Clark's mention that the Vollstedt-Ford Indycar he had driven at Riverside had been tried with a rudimentary wing – in the form of a tray over the high exhaust system. Leo Wybrott, who was Clark's mechanic in those races 'down under', takes up the story, which involves helicopters and a pilot called Roger Porteous, who was the brother of Lotus mechanic Dale Porteous.

'Roger and I went out to an airport where helicopters were kept for wild deer hunting. They used to fly so close to the rocks that they were always clipping rotor blades, so there was a ready supply of helicopter blades. We drove back to Christchurch with a long section of helicopter blade hanging out of the back window.

'We tried to optimise downforce versus the amount of drag, came up with a supposed figure, and ended up with this wing mounted on the gearbox for the next race, at Invercargill. We painted it red, put a Firestone sticker on it and had it on the car for the first practice. I am not at all sure Jimmy ran properly with it, but there is quite a lot of evidence that he did some laps and said he thought it helped a little bit. With end-plates on it, though, it would have been so much more effective. Anyway, we decided that we would not use it in the race because we knew that Colin would not be too hot on that. However, Giovanni Marelli, who was running Chris Amon's Ferrari, photographed it, and that led to one of the first wings on a Formula 1 car being on a Ferrari.'

Wybrott and Dale Porteous subsequently gave this heavy wing to Classic Team Lotus and it reappeared, this time on R10, during the weekend of the 2013 Goodwood Revival, for, as Clive Chapman stated, 'a bit of fun'.

For Team Lotus the wing age really started at Rouen for the French Grand Prix. There the 49Bs were fitted with strutted aerofoils that acted directly upon the rear suspension uprights, converting maximum download to pure traction; Chapman calculated 400lb download at 150mph, although this was never put to the test. The science of racing car wings was not yet fully understood and Jackie Oliver became the first Lotus victim of the concept when, edging his Type 49 into another's slipstream, he felt his car slither away from him. The resulting accident was a massive one but the monocoque stood up well to the impact and Oliver was able to walk away, white-faced but unharmed.

The look of the Type 49s became even more bizarre the following season with the fitting of a second strutted aerofoil acting on the front suspension uprights. Doug Nye coined the term bi-wing to describe these cars with full-width aerofoils front and rear, pointing out that the name biplane, which some had adopted, conjured up images of early aircraft with one wing above the other. At the 1969 Spanish Grand Prix the 49s appeared with the tallest and widest wings yet seen on the car. These

were skinned in aluminium over an inadequate number of section formers, their surfaces being unbraced mid-span. The struts could not accept the negative loading that occurred as the cars traversed a particularly vicious hump and the wings of both cars collapsed.

It was normal to use fixed mountings, with the wing incidence set on assembly or at least when the car was stationary. A rear wing that could be feathered by the driver, however, was fitted for the 1968 Mexican Grand Prix. The driver had an extra foot pedal to the left of the clutch that he could press while on the straights

LEFT A second strutted aerofoil first appeared on the Lotus 49s at the 1969 South African Grand Prix. (Ford)

RIGHT Donington's Lotus 49 has the three-tier rear wing that was developed for the Lotus 72 and used for the 49 in 1970. Behind stands an example of the excesses of 1968 and 1969. *(Author)*

BELOW The cockpit of R8. *(Author)*

and this action, by means of a Bowden cable, would cause the wing to be flattened into a neutral position in order to reduce drag. As he approached a corner, the driver would naturally move his left foot back to the clutch pedal and tensioned bungee cords would then bring the aerofoil down to its normal attack angle, thereby helping both to slow down the car and to assist traction out of the corner.

After the Spanish Grand Prix debacle, the Commission Sportive Internationale (CSI) placed a temporary ban on wings. Team Lotus's improvised answer at Monaco was to fashion a low-mounted, scoop-shaped panel above the gearbox using interior panelling from its transporters – the Lotus mechanics were nothing if not resourceful! – while keeping the nose vanes in place.

New aerofoil regulations came into force for the Dutch Grand Prix, leading to a rear wing 'look' that was to remain largely unaltered for many years, although a three-tier version, developed for the Type 72, was fitted to the 49 in 1970. The new rules stipulated a maximum height of 80cm (31.5in) above the underside of the car and a maximum overall width of 110cm (43.3in) behind the rear axle line. The wing had to be mounted on a sprung part of the chassis.

Cockpit

The cockpit was formed by the 'belling out' of a section of the inner sheets and the insertion of two bulkheads with rounded corner fillets, one forming the seat backrest and the other supporting the dash panel. Through a hole in the forward bulkhead projected the steering column carrying a 'trademark' Lotus steering wheel with a leather-trimmed rim, the leather initially in red but later black. The steering wheel was offset to the left by an inch in order to provide space for the driver to use the right-hand gear-change. The gear-change linkage had a simple ball-jointed lower end and no lever gate.

A Perspex two-piece air deflector screen surrounded the cockpit. Its design was familiar, being similar to the style first adopted in 1963 as a development to the Lotus 25 and then featuring on the Type 33 as well as Formula 2 and Indianapolis cars. With this type of screen, the driver had a clear view over the top of it, but the screen still produced a curtain of air pressure strong enough to deflect raindrops and insects.

The dash featured, from left to right, a combined oil pressure/temperature gauge, rev

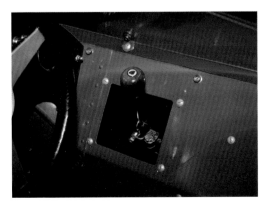

ABOVE The steering wheel, originally red, is offset to the left to provide space for the driver to change gear. *(Author)*

FAR LEFT The cockpit is surrounded by the distinctive two-piece windscreen used by Lotus through the mid-1960s. *(Author)*

LEFT Rear of the dash on R7. *(Author)*

FAR LEFT The battery is located beneath the driver's knees. *(Author)*

FAR LEFT The gear lever has no gate. *(Author)*

LEFT Having suffered an accident in which his right hand was severely damaged, Geoff Farmer, current owner of R7, had his car fitted with a smaller-than-standard gear lever knob. *(Author)*

counter, water temperature gauge, fuel pump switch, ignition switch, fuel pressure gauge and ammeter. The battery was located beneath the driver's knees.

Seat harnesses were not in use in Formula 1 when the Lotus 49 was introduced although in the USA they had been used in Indianapolis-style racing for some years. There was still a feeling in some quarters that, as the drivers were sitting surrounded by fuel, it might be better to be thrown out in the event of an accident. Following his experience in the 1966 Belgian Grand Prix when he crashed his BRM in the wet and became trapped in it, Jackie Stewart began a vigorous campaign to make motor racing safer. The following year, at the German Grand Prix, he was the first to use a full safety harness in a grand prix car.

Safety harnesses became mandatory in Formula 1 in 1969 and were therefore installed in the Lotus 49s. Their worth was surely indicated later that year, at Watkins Glen, when Graham Hill crashed. Early in the race, having spun and been forced to push-start his car, he had been unable to buckle up his belts afterwards. Rather than immediately return to the pits, he stayed out and suffered a tyre deflation, which caused the car to hit an earth bank and become pitched into a series of rolls. Hill was thrown out, breaking one leg and damaging the other. Recovery from his injuries took a long time and he was never as competitive again.

Apertures were let into the side of the cockpit to give the driver elbow room. During 1967 Team Lotus had difficulties in making

RIGHT In 1969 it became obligatory to fit a safety harness in a Formula 1 car. *(Author)*

FAR RIGHT R10 features a period head rest. *(Author)*

RIGHT The pedals in R12. *(Author)*

FAR RIGHT Holes were let in the side of the cockpit to give the driver elbow room. *(Author)*

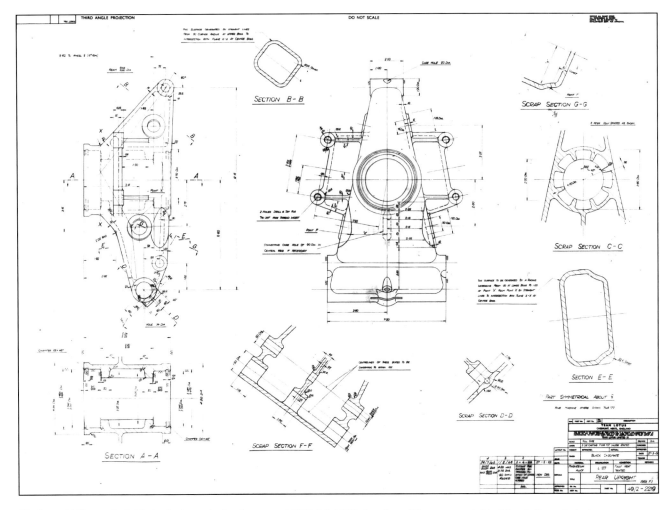

SECTION B-B

SCRAP SECTION G-G

SCRAP SECTION C-C

SECTION E-E

PART SYMMETRICAL ABOUT ℄

SCRAP SECTION D-D

SECTION A-A

SCRAP SECTION F-F

Clark and Hill comfortable in their cockpits, for they had rather different requirements. Clark drove in a very reclined position, his arms out straight, while Hill, a larger man, sat more upright and needed room to move his arms.

Steering and suspension

The all-round independent suspension, with its built-in anti-dive geometry, was typical Lotus. Cast-alloy top arms, which actuated inboard Armstrong coil spring/damper units, were tucked out of the airstream each side of the footbox. Longer, revised rocker arm fairings were used from R3 onwards, R1 being modified in this way when the new bulkhead was fitted after the 1967 British Grand Prix. The front rocker arms were again revised for the 1969 German Grand Prix, now being straight instead of angled slightly upwards; this provided increased suspension travel, an important factor at the undulating Nürburgring. A fabricated lower link was jointed

ABOVE A 1968 drawing of the rear upright. *(Classic Team Lotus)*

BELOW The rocker arms contained seating for the top swivel bearings. This Brian Hatton drawing also shows the quickly detachable anti-roll bar with its expanding square ends. *(LAT Photographic)*

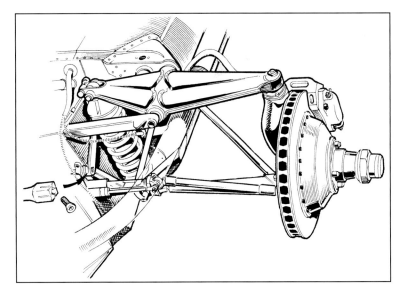

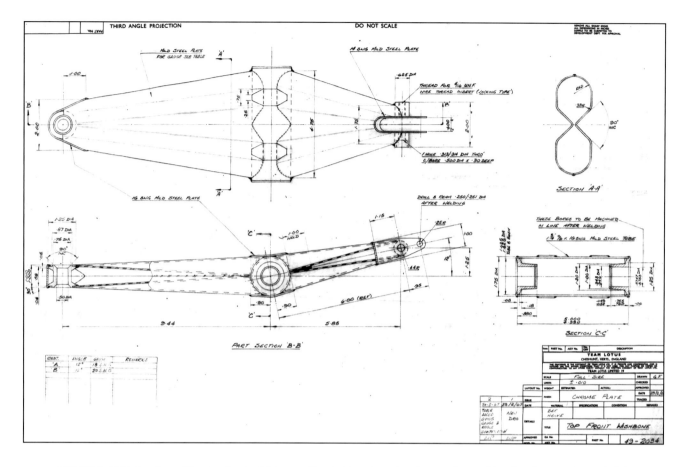

ABOVE A 1967 drawing of the top front wishbone. *(Classic Team Lotus)*

BELOW Rear suspension transverse links were attached to the engine by tubular subframes, each bolted to the engine at four points. *(LAT Photographic)*

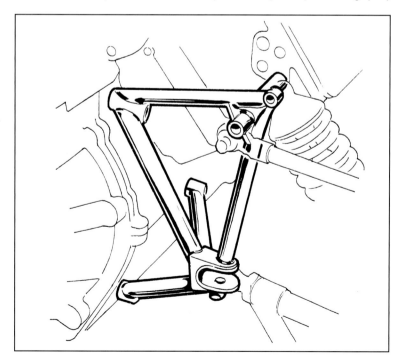

to a radius rod leading from an inward pick-up, which was buried back on the hull.

The location of the rear suspension featured top links, reversed lower wishbones, twin radius rods (feeding drive and braking torques into the rear corners of the monocoque) and an anti-roll bar. The inclined, outboard-mounted coil spring/damper units were ahead of the axle.

The strength of the tapered front suspension top rocker arms proved to be insufficient and twice during the 1967 season they were beefed up. After Hill's loss of the lead in that year's British Grand Prix, when an Allen screw fell out of the rear suspension, the mounting for the top link was twice modified; the rear radius rod pick-up point was also strengthened. At the end of the year, stronger rear suspension subframes, which bolted on to the rear of the engine heads and block, were adopted.

OPPOSITE TOP Lower rear wishbone, as drawn in 1967. *(Classic Team Lotus)*

OPPOSITE BOTTOM The rear anti-roll bar. *(Classic Team Lotus)*

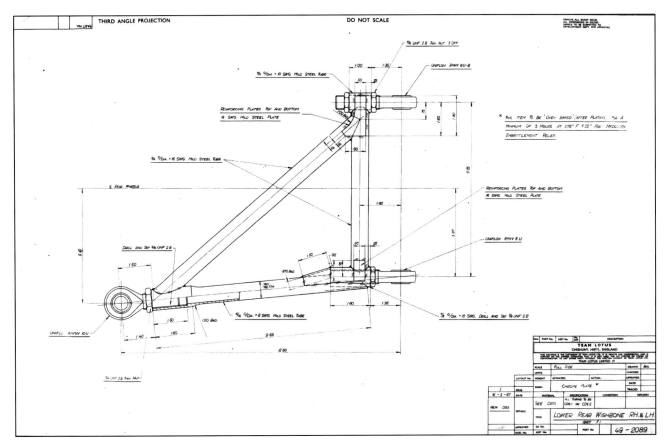

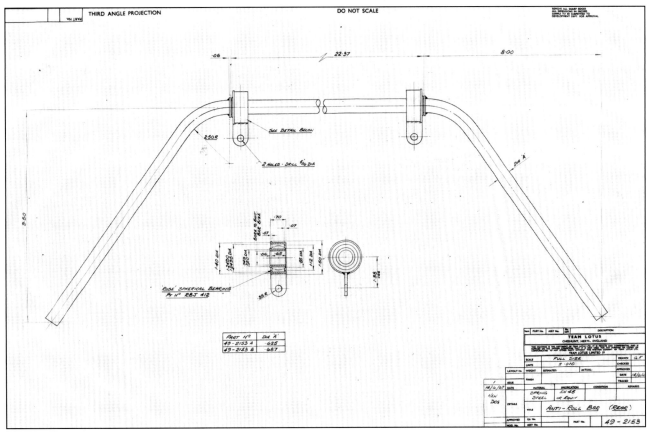

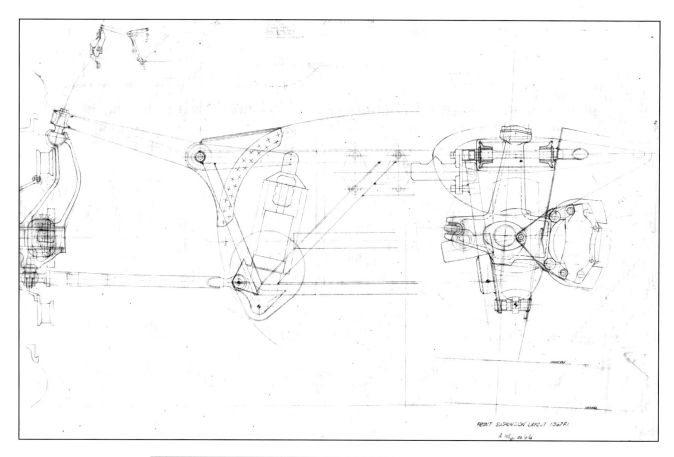

FRONT SUSPENSION LAYOUT 1967 F.1.

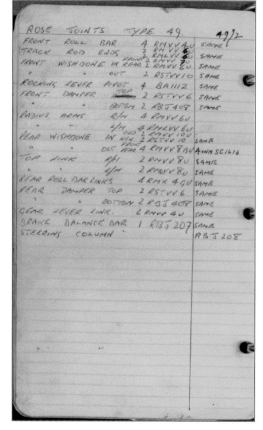

Jim Clark's mechanic, Allan McCall, reccounts a personal experience concerning a suspension failure at the end of the 1967 season: 'After the embarrassment of the rear top link breaking in the USA, as soon as I arrived in Mexico City I made a strengthening bracket that I fitted to R2. I even had it nickel-plated at my own expense. This was not the done thing: Chapman took one look at my brace and told Jim to drive the spare car. I guess I good as handed in my notice – I needed to be shown it was not required and he was right of course. I got Moises Solana, who did a good job running with the leaders with R2 until the motor dumped. If you look at video footage of the 1967 Mexican GP you can see my bracket on Solana's car.'

As part of the attempt to reduce sliding following the introduction of wider tyres in early 1968, the suspension geometry of R5 was altered for the Race of Champions. There were new rear uprights, with less projection over the hub level, and a lower top radius rod mounting. When R5 was rebuilt to 49B specification, its wheelbase was lengthened by raking the front suspension arms three inches (7.5cm) forward –

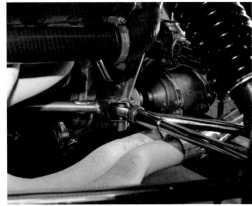

FAR LEFT The front suspension of R10, showing the top rocker arm and lower A-arm with angled trailing edge to oppose braking forces. *(Author)*

LEFT The forward inboard mount for the rear lower A-arm. *(Author)*

LEFT The spring and adjustable damper, also showing the top of the control arm and two radius arms. *(Author)*

RIGHT In order to put more weight over the rear wheels, the front wheels were moved forward by 2in on the Type 49B; the oil tank was also moved to the rear. *(Author)*

BELOW The original design of top front rocker, not swept forward; the early, vee-shaped oil tank is also seen. *(Andy Brown)*

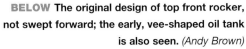

BELOW The fabricated beam designed to take the spring and top suspension. *(Author)*

ABOVE The later, swept-forward rocker arm, on R7. *(Author)*

BELOW Inboard detail of the front suspension on R3, also showing where the radiator air exited on the early Type 49 – hence the slight flare to the rear of the nose cone at this point. The 'coil-over' spring/damper is clearly visible, showing the top attachment to the inboard end of the top front rocker. Also visible is the front anti-roll bar lever arm, and below this is the outboard end of the steering rack and the track rod. Two flexible hoses for oil (braided steel) and water (rubber) can also be seen. *(Andy Brown)*

with the effect of putting more load on the 49's rear end – and the lower rear radius rod pick-ups were resited closer to the car's centreline axis. With the changes made to the 49B, the engine's cylinder heads were relieved of carrying the suspension loads direct.

For the car's final year in grands prix, 1970, the suspension was modified with new front uprights and suspension geometry to account for the fitting of new 13in front wheels and tyres. This led to the four cars that were so modified – R6, R7, R8 and R10 – being designated 49Cs.

The rack-and-pinion steering was originally supplied by Alford & Alder but changed to Cam Gears for the 49B. From the 1968 French Grand Prix there was a further steering set-up that featured a rack-and-pinion system derived from that of the Ford Escort; this used helical gears and was said to have a smoother action and slightly quicker ratio.

Brakes

At the front, cast uprights initially supported ventilated Kelsey-Hayes brake discs (12in/30cm diameter, 1.5in/4cm width) that originated from the Ford Thunderbird, with four-piston Girling calipers using Lotus-designed alloy bridge pieces. Two bracing struts were fitted between each caliper and a point near the centre of the upright to alleviate occasional wedging of the pads. The brakes were mounted well inboard of the wheels and therefore were exposed to direct airflow.

The rear featured massive brake calipers behind the axle, front and rear, clasping thick ventilated discs. Girling AR-type calipers were introduced on the 49B.

The heavily ventilated discs had a tendency to over-cool and glaze their pads, which would then lose their bite. Softer pad materials were at first tried but it was not long before the ventilated discs were abandoned, to be replaced by thinner, solid discs that offered more consistent temperatures. With a width of $3/8$ in, the solid discs were considerably more slender than the ventilated ones. The first time they were used was on Clark's car, R2, at the 1967 German Grand Prix, and they became the regular fitment on all 49s from Canada onwards.

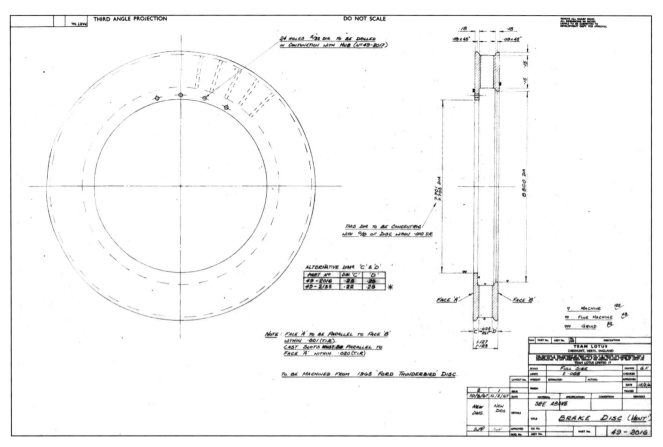

THIRD ANGLE PROJECTION   DO NOT SCALE

24 HOLES 5/32 DIA. TO BE DRILLED
IN CONJUNCTION WITH HUB (N° 49-2017)

ALTERNATIVE DIMS 'C' & 'D'

PART N°	DIM 'C'	'D'
49-2016	·25	·25
49-2133	·22	·28

THIS DIA. TO BE CONCENTRIC
WITH O/D OF DISC WITHIN ·010 T.I.R.

NOTE: FACE 'A' TO BE PARALLEL TO FACE 'B'
WITHIN ·001 (T.I.R.).
CAST SLOTS MUST BE PARALLEL TO
FACE 'A' WITHIN ·020 (T.I.R.)

TO BE MACHINED FROM 1965 'FORD THUNDERBIRD' DISC.

FACE 'A'   FACE 'B'

▽ MACHINE
▽▽ FINE MACHINE
▽▽▽ GRIND

TEAM LOTUS
CHESHUNT, HERTS, ENGLAND

TITLE BRAKE DISC (VENT)
PART N° 49-2016

ABOVE The brake discs were ventilated on earlier cars. *(Classic Team Lotus)*

FAR LEFT Non-ventilated discs, as seen here on R3, soon replaced ventilated ones. *(Andy Brown)*

LEFT Non-ventilated disc brake on R10, with single-pot trailing caliper. *(Author)*

FAR LEFT This shows the brake 'hat' or disc-mounting shell; the disc is rigidly mounted. *(Author)*

LEFT Inside face of a disc, showing front upright. *(Author)*

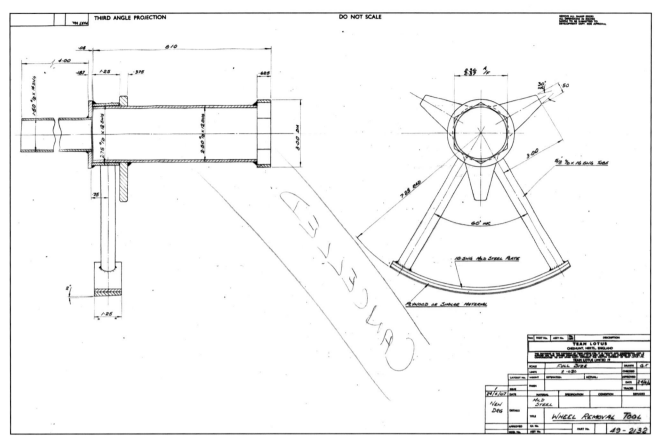

ABOVE The deep dish of the wheel meant that it required a special removal tool. *(Classic Team Lotus)*

RIGHT The National Motor Museum acquired its wheel-removal tool as part of the package when it purchased R3. *(Author)*

ABOVE RIGHT Wheel on R3. *(Author)*

RIGHT Front wheel on R7. *(Author)*

FAR RIGHT Rear wheel on R12. *(Author)*

Wheels and tyres

The 15in diameter wheels were cast magnesium of Lotus manufacture. The front rims were originally 8in wide, increased to 10in for the final two races of 1967. The deep rim meant that a special tool had to be used to reach the wheel nut.

Experience with wider, new-generation Firestone tyres during the early part of the 1968 season showed that more rearward weight bias would be an advantage. Loadings had decreased as the tyre contact patches had increased and, under most conditions, the more lightly loaded tyres were more prone to sliding despite the fact that they were wider. In addition to the huge, saddle oil tank first fitted to R5 at the Race of Champions and a change in suspension geometry, new, 12in wide, deep-cone wheels were fitted, still of 15in diameter. The rear tyres of the 49B, as it had now become, were 15in wide across the shoulders.

Firestone's sticky Y-construction, B11-compound tyres were introduced in 1968.

These removed an element of driveline cushioning, leading to halfshaft failure.

Thanks to problems in the development of the Lotus 72, the Type 49 was still in service during part of 1970. That year, Firestone developed a new 13in front tyre that was used on the car, which was now known as the 49C.

Engine

The four-cam, 90° V8 Cosworth DFV engine was, in effect, the basis of the Lotus 49 as the engine and chassis were created in harmony. The DFV ('Double Four Valve') was designed to be particularly short so that it effectively fitted into the chassis package. The crankcase carried the chassis loads between the back of the monocoque and the gearbox. The ancillaries were placed on the side of the block to shorten the package. Designer Keith Duckworth believed that the mechanical efficiency of a V8 would be better than that of a 12-cylinder even though most of his rivals felt the latter to be the future.

The engine was attached to the back of the

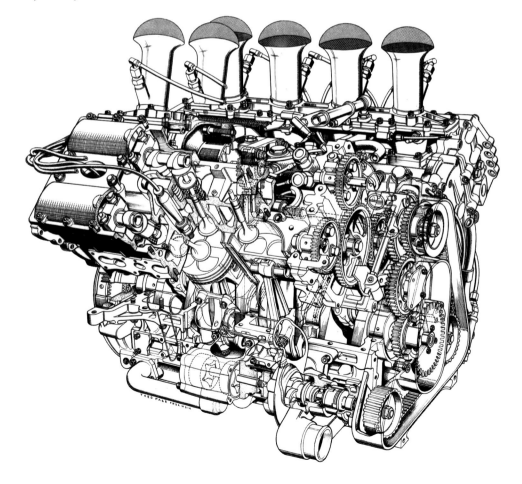

LEFT Theo Page's 1967 cutaway drawing clearly shows the workings of the Cosworth DFV. *(Ford)*

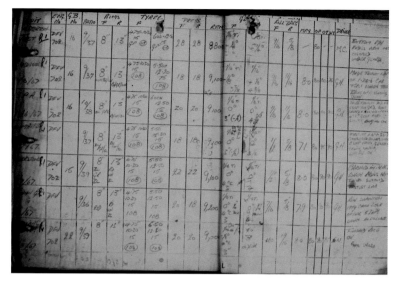

ABOVE Bob Dance's notebook indicates that DFV number 702 was used in R1 during 1967.

ABOVE RIGHT A Cosworth DFV on display in the National Motor Museum. *(Andy Brown)*

RIGHT Cosworth DFV front casting. *(Author)*

RIGHT The starter motor on R3. *(Author)*

RIGHT Exhaust mounting on R3. *(Author)*

monocoque by just four bolts, two through the front face of the sump and one through each of the outer cam covers – the absolute minimum. Former grand prix driver Martin Brundle, who demonstrated a Lotus 49 many years later at Silverstone, observed that its engine was 10 years ahead of the chassis.

'They all gave over 400bhp but the highest was 407,' observed Duckworth's partner, Mike Costin, of the engine in 1967 specification. 'We did not do specials. We thought it was impossible to test within plus or minus one per cent.'

A destroked 2½-litre version, known as the DFW, was built for use in the Tasman series. This was considered a relatively straightforward conversion, using a short-stroke crankshaft to reduce capacity to 2,495cc, and longer connecting rods to keep friction down and compression ratio up. When the Tasman series was over, it was a simple matter of putting back the standard rods, pistons and crank. The DFW had a bore of 85.67mm and a stroke of 54.10mm, and delivered an estimated power output of 350bhp at 9,200rpm.

There were two things wrong with the DFV at the design stage. One was the design of the oil scavenge system, the other the lack of torsional accommodation in the gear drive to the camshafts. Mike Costin believed that the problem with the scavenge system should have been resolved at the design stage but that the gear-drive problem had been impossible to predict. It nearly robbed the engine of its first win and was to be a continuing issue in the DFV's early career.

Because the oil drains from the cylinder head were too small, oil collected in the cylinder heads at high revs, emerging from the breathers instead of draining back to the sump for collection by the scavenge pumps. The internal breathing was eventually sorted out but the early DFVs had to be fitted with large external breathing tubes connected to tin boxes on the right-hand cam cover.

Although the DFV engine won first time out, there was obviously a need to improve its power delivery. The DFV originally had a hole at 5,000rpm and then came out of it sharply; Jim Clark described it as like suddenly having two engines. A massive horsepower or torque change happened in just a few revs, making the car a handful to control. In response Chapman and Phillippe designed a little progressive throttle pedal linkage to help overcome the problem and this was used by Clark until Cosworth produced a cam linkage at the throttle slides that had the same effect.

The cost of a Cosworth DFV during 1967 was £7,500. During the life of the Lotus 49 all DFVs had to be returned to Cosworth for rebuild or repair, a rule that was relaxed by 1971. The service interval was about 500 miles and the work would routinely involve stripping the engine. Pistons, valve springs and oil pump internals would be replaced; if the engine had been over-revved, the big-end bolts would also be replaced. Other components would be crack-tested and inspected. Coils were replaced every 12 months. The work would be followed by dynamometer tests and an inspection that included an endoscope check of the combustion chambers.

Block

The Cosworth DFV was based on an LM 8 WP heat-treated aluminium-alloy block with a five-main-bearing crank. The alloy was reasonably easy to cast and had excellent machining properties. The blocks were cast in Worcester at Cosworth's own foundry, where the company employed a special casting process that enabled it to produce an aluminium block that matched the strength of a cast-iron one. The block extends from the decks to the centreline of the crankshaft, the lower half of the crankcase being integral with the sump casing.

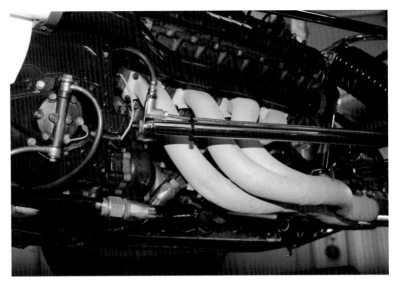

The front, centre and rear main bearing caps are formed by the sump/lower crankcase and numbers two and four bearings have conventional bolted caps; early engines, however, had five sump bearings. The caps are aligned with one dowel either side and tightened regularly so that the gap between cap and block remains square. When this is achieved the dowels are locked, the feeler gauge is slid out and both sides are slowly torqued. A hole underneath the metering unit allows for any leakage, such as fuel or water, to go through the right-hand cylinder bank.

ABOVE The exhaust system of R3. Also clearly shown are the oil pump and the brake line that leads along the lower radius arm to the caliper. *(Author)*

BELOW DFV block (in need of repair) and head. *(Author)*

ABOVE Flat-plane crankshaft, con rod, piston and cylinder liner. *(Author)*

Cylinder liners

The limited metallurgical development of the time meant that use of an aluminium block required cast-iron cylinder liners to be fitted, originally in 'wet' form, meaning that they are in constant contact with water. The liners are sealed by two O-rings at the bottom and Cooper's mechanical joints at the top.

The block is cleaned and prepared prior to fitting of the liners, all of which are marked to show their correct position within the block. To receive the liners, which have to be seated a precise distance from the top of the block, the block is heated to 150°C. Sealing between the cylinder head and the block is secured by a Cooper ring located in a recess formed between the liner and the block. Grooves machined on top of the block at the edge between the liners gave an indication of leaks. In the event of a blow-up, it is possible to fit liners of bigger external diameter but standard bore by machining their locations in the block.

Crankshaft

The Laystall nitrided M 40B forged-steel crankshaft is of a single-plane shape, mounted low to keep the centre of gravity low. At one end a boss takes the flywheel with eight $^3/_8$ in UNF bolts. At the other end is the location for the timing gear.

The crankshaft revolves in five steel-backed Vandervell main bearings with lead-indium wear surfaces, numbers two and four holding it in position. It has five journals, and four pins with two con rods mounted next to each other on each pin. At the timing end, the crank gear drives a series of further gears; the main gear is secured by a press fit and located on one dowel.

Conventional oil seals are used. On the front of the engine the oil seal is pushed into the front timing gear cover and secured by three screws. On the flywheel side the oil seal is secured by a retaining ring.

Con rods

The design of the con rods and pistons follows the same lines as the Cosworth FVA Formula 2 engine. The con rods are forged steel, split across the big ends at 90° to the rod shank, the outside being shot-peened for extra strength. In the little end there is a mixture of soft metal alloy. On the big end there is a plain shell bearing held by a cup and two $^3/_8$ in UNC high-tensile bolts. The tightening of the con rods is conventional.

Pistons

The forged aluminium pistons are each retained on the con rod by a gudgeon pin, which is retained by two circlips. Between pin and circlips are dished synthetic washers known as Belleville washers. The piston crown is pocketed to give clearance to the valves. Three piston rings are used, two compression and one oil control.

Cylinder heads

The heat-treated aluminium-alloy cylinder heads have aluminium, bronze and copper-nickel valve seats and guides. The heads are interchangeable between the cylinder banks. The inlet ports are inclined towards the centre of the engine on both cylinder banks, the exhaust ports to the outside. The ports to each combustion chamber merge into a single inlet tract inside the head.

On the front of the cylinder head is an idler

RIGHT Close-up of the head, with valves and springs. *(Author)*

gear that drives the camshaft gears mounted on a roller bearing on a steel pin that protrudes from the cylinder head. All the valves are assembled with double springs held to the valves by a top cap with two collets. Sealing of the valve stem to the valve guide is by a rubbery seal that is held against the stem by a spring, which is secured in turn to the guide by the bottom spring platform.

Ten studs hold each cylinder head to the block, with four smaller studs on each outside edge. There are two 1.36in (34.5mm) diameter inlet valves and two 1.14in (29mm) diameter exhaust valves per cylinder, with 32° included angle and 0.41in (10mm) lift.

Cam carriers

The cam carriers are each retained by ten studs, which also retain the cam bearings, and by eight cap screws. The cam carrier carries the tappet pistons and camshafts in their own assembly. A small shim is located between each valve stem and tappet bucket; shims and buckets are made from steel.

Camshaft

Two gear-driven overhead camshafts for each cylinder bank rest on plain shell bearings and five caps, which are numbered to avoid being incorrectly replaced; at first the camshafts were cast iron but later they were made of tuftrided steel. Although the inlet and exhaust cams are the same shape, they cannot be wrongly installed because of the differing distances between the lobes arising from the inlet and exhaust valves having different diameters. At the rear of the front bearing is a shoulder that prevents the camshaft from moving longitudinally.

Two magnesium plates seal the rear of the cylinder head and the cam carrier, one secured to the cylinder head by four ¼in UNC bolt cap heads and a 5⁄16in UNC cap head with a big washer, the other bolted to the cam carrier in like fashion.

The cam cover is cast in magnesium and bolted to the carrier by twenty two 5⁄16in UNF cap heads around its edge and ten 5⁄16in nuts and washers down its centre. The front part of the cover is designed to form part of the engine mounting. Four 5⁄16in bolts secure an engine plate to the cover, which is fixed to the chassis

ABOVE Camshaft. *(Author)*

by a single 3⁄8in UNF bolt. An aluminium mounting block is located at the bottom of the sump and bolted to the chassis by two $^3/_8$ in studs.

To lubricate the cam, an oil passage passes through the cylinder head from the block to the centre camshaft bearing. The camshaft being hollow, this allows the oil to pass to the other bearings as well.

Throttle slides

The throttle slides rest on a series of rollers and ball bearings, the travel being limited by plastic stops. The slide is returned by two springs located on the back of the manifold and supported by two plastic plungers. These springs are assisted by two additional ones that are mounted to suit different throttle/pedal arrangements.

Inlet trumpets

The gauze-covered, conical-shaped inlet trumpets are supported by the manifold top, as is the throttle control rod. They are mounted on two O-rings and retained by a steel ring that is screwed to the manifold top. The fuel injector is located in the trumpet.

BELOW Throttle slides. *(Author)*

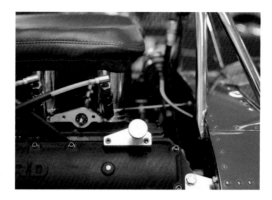

Metering unit

The metering unit and the electrical assembly
are connected to a small gearbox that obtains
its power from the second compound gear via
a quill shaft. This means that the timing of the
ignition and fuel injection can be accurately set
in relation to each other. The unit is located
inside the vee, the front of the metering unit
being supported by an aluminium mount bolted
to the block.

Looking from the front, the layout of
the timing gears follows the shape of the
engine. The crankshaft gear drives the first
compound gear, which in turn drives the
second compound gear. This provides the
take-off point for the metering unit/ignition
assembly drive and carries on the timing gear
to the camshafts via idler gears. The second
compound gear is a complex assembly made
up of a hub incorporating 12 miniature torsion
bars. At the end of the line are the camshaft
gears, bolted to the camshaft by three cap
screws. A cast magnesium cover on the engine
and two smaller magnesium covers on each
cylinder head assembly enclose these gears.

On each corner of the cast cover is a pulley
that carries a toothed belt driven by the second
compound gear to provide the power for the
engine's ancillary equipment. The mechanical
fuel pump, water pump for the left-hand bank
and oil pressure pump are on the left-hand side.
The water pump for the right-hand bank and
the scavenge pump are on the right-hand side;
between the rear of this water pump and the
front of the scavenge pump is a small clutch
assembly that slips at a pre-set load, thus
preventing damage to the rotors of the scavenge
pump and drive belt when the oil is cold.

Water pumps

The two centrifugal water pumps, one
each side of the crankcase, are identical in
construction apart from the fact that they are
handed and cannot be interchanged. The
impeller is contained in the aluminium housing
of the pump body and its shaft is supported
by two ball bearings. Water from the pumps is

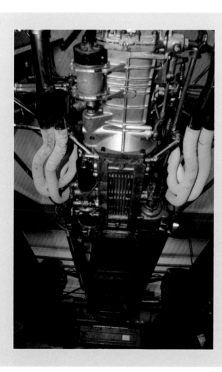

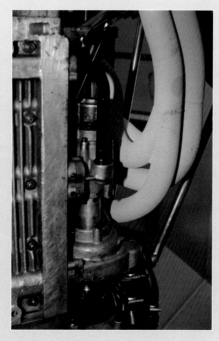

passed through an aluminium tube secured to the block by a cast-aluminium elbow. The tube is sealed to the elbow and to the pump outlet with rubber O-rings.

Oil pressure pump

The oil pressure pump body is mounted to the engine. It contains the rotor, pressure-relief valve and oil filter in one assembly. The pumping mechanism is a conventional eccentric rotor type. Oil is passed from the pump to the engine via a pipe, excess oil from the pressure-relief valve being bled into the scavenge system. The pump receives its power through an Oldhams coupling from the rear of the left-hand water pump.

Engine oil system

Oil is drawn from the tank into the oil pump, where it is pressurised and pumped through the filter into the cylinder block via a steel tube. It passes through oilways in the block to the crankshaft assembly, the cylinder heads and camshaft assemblies, with a small amount being directed on to the compound gears through a small jet. Oil collects in the sump and is scavenged and returned to the tank via oil coolers. The oil tank is vented to a catch tank.

The scavenging system was reckoned to be superior to that of other Formula 1 engines of the time. The approximate consumption for a grand prix was about six pints.

Water system

The water pumps are connected by a passage in the sump that enables water to be introduced into either pump. The water is pumped by the impellers in the cylinder block, passes around the liners and through the cylinder head, and leaves the engine through an outlet at the rear of each head. It returns to the pumps having been cooled through the radiators. A thin aluminium cover protects the belt and pulley arrangement.

Fuel system

An electrical high-pressure pump sucks five-star petrol through a filter, then to a non-return valve or bypasses the mechanic engine fuel pump, then to another filter and the metering unit that distributes the fuel to the cylinders through injectors.

LEFT The fuel filter on R10. (Author)

COSWORTH DFV ENGINE SPECIFICATION

Configuration 90° V8
Capacity 2,993cc
Bore 3.373in
Stroke 2.555in
Compression ratio 11:1 (approx)
Maximum power 408bhp at 9,000rpm, rising to 415bhp at 9,500rpm in 1968 and 430bhp at 10,000rpm in 1969–70
Maximum torque 245lb ft at 8,500rpm
Valve lift 0.410in (less tappet clearance)
Timing Inlet/exhaust 102° MOP
Firing order 1–8–3–6–4–5–2–7
Cylinder configuration (from front) 5/1, 6/2, 7/3, 8/4
Cylinder block Cast aluminium alloy; general assembly is bearing type
Wet liners Cast iron in constant contact with water
Crankshaft Steel; five main bearings; positioned between block and sump
Con rods forged steel (shot-peened)
Pistons Forged aluminium with two compression rings and one oil control ring
Ancillary system Two water pumps, one per side; one oil pressure pump; one scavenge pump
Cylinder heads Cast aluminium alloy; two 1.14in exhaust valves and two 1.36in inlet valves per cylinder, assembled with double springs; one spark plug per cylinder located in centre of combustion chamber
Inlet manifold Cast aluminium alloy; inlet trumpets press-formed steel with injector location
Cam carriers Cast aluminium alloy, taking the tappet piston and camshaft
Throttle slides Steel sliding on a series of ball bearings and rollers returned by two guided springs
Camshafts Four (initially) cast iron, each turns on five bearings
Cam covers Magnesium casting
Injection system Lucas indirect injection shuttle metering system; pressure approx 110psi; injection timing at 30° ATDC
Ignition system Lucas OPUS ignition with Thyristor engine speed limiter; Lucas alternator
Spark plugs Autolite or Ford, 10mm
Weight 165kg

Fuel injection system

Use is made of the indirect Lucas shuttle metering system. A separate electric pump is mounted on the chassis and governed by a dashboard switch. This sucks the petrol from the tank, sending it around the system. The petrol is pressurised because of its flow and by a relief valve designed to keep the pressure at around 110psi. The fuel is fed to a metering unit, which combines a metering distributor with a mixture control unit. A piston, driven by the shaft, coming from the distribution located inside the metering unit, sends the correct amount of fuel at the precise time to each cylinder. The amount injected is determined by the travel of a small free piston, or shuttle, operated by the fuel pressure.

The mixture control assembly is a simple fuel cam mounted on the front of the unit and liaised to the slides of the engine by a small rod. When opening, the slide determines the travel of the shuttle, sending the quantity of fuel to be injected. The engine also receives the exact amount of fuel to match the quantity of air admitted. The metered fuel reaches the cylinders through injectors located on the outside of the trumpets that atomise the fuel as it enters the air stream. The shuttle or fuel cam is mounted on an eccentric pin going through it. This has five positions and initially is set in full-rich position when cold.

A different set of fuel cam profiles was available to suit varying race tracks, especially with respect to altitude.

Ignition system

The static Lucas ignition components were carried on the gearbox and on early DFVs were open to the elements. It had been thought that this location, well away from the exhaust system, made the installation easily accessible.

The components include the pulse amplifier and relay for the Lucas engine speed limiter, which is actuated by a serrated disc and pick-up on the front of the crankshaft, causing a complete break in ignition above a predetermined speed. This speed is easily adjustable by a potentiometer device.

BELOW Drawing of the 16swg aluminium electrics tray.
(Classic Team Lotus)

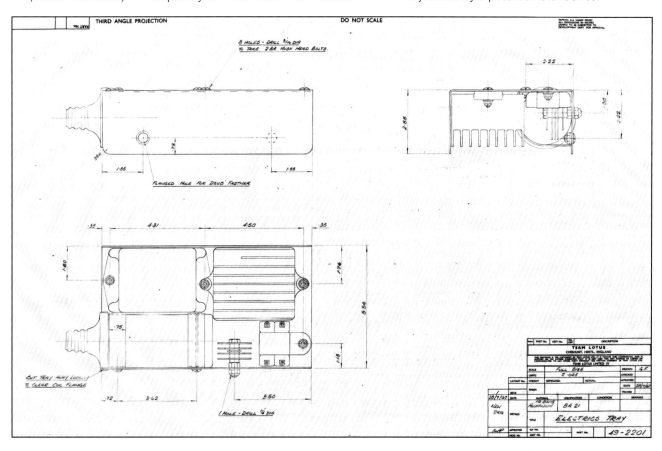

ABOVE The electrics were located in the centre of the vee; in the days before air boxes each fuel injection trumpet was protected by a gauze cover. *(Author)*

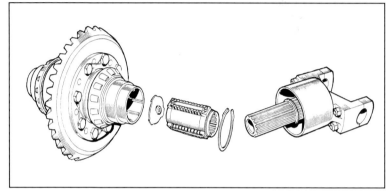

Transmission

At first, a specially tailored, light, uprated ZF 5DS12 synchromesh gearbox with five forward gears and reverse was installed. This incorporated sliding-spline joints within its output shafts in each side. Colin Chapman was initially very enthusiastic about the ZF 'box, which was very much lighter than the Hewland transmission used by most of the other teams, but engine designers Keith Duckworth and Mike Costin were not convinced.

The ZF's weaknesses became apparent at the 1967 French Grand Prix, held on the Bugatti circuit, which used part of the Le Mans 24 Hours track. The ZF looked slab-sided and its flat sides flexed slightly with the stop/go nature of this rather 'Mickey Mouse' circuit, causing failures of the crown wheel and pinion on both Lotus 49s, which had been running first and second until this happened. The gearbox was immediately modified with large cross-bolted side plates fitted as a temporary expedient. Although this stop-gap gearbox was used to win the British Grand Prix, a redesigned heavier,

TOP Rear view of the Lucas electrics. *(Author)*

ABOVE Brian Hatton's 1967 exploded view of the final drive showing three-row roller splines built into the original ZF gearbox. The spline barrel fitted on to conventional splines, which were used to ease manufacture and assembly. *(LAT Photographic)*

LEFT Underside of ZF gearbox. *(Author)*

ABOVE Left-hand side of the ZF gearbox, with starter motor alongside. The way in which the anti-roll bar was adjusted, by sliding clamps fore and aft, is clearly visible. *(Author)*

ABOVE RIGHT The rear of the ZF gearbox was protected. *(Author)*

BELOW The frame holding the exhaust pipes also helped to protect the ZF gearbox on the early Type 49s. *(Classic Team Lotus)*

stronger casing was then introduced, but its extra weight nullified the ZF's advantage over a Hewland 'box.

A downside of the ZF 'box was that it featured fixed intermediate ratios and final drives. Thus, ratios could only be changed with a near-total strip-down. Previously Team Lotus had tended to overcome this shortcoming by taking a number of ready-assembled gearboxes

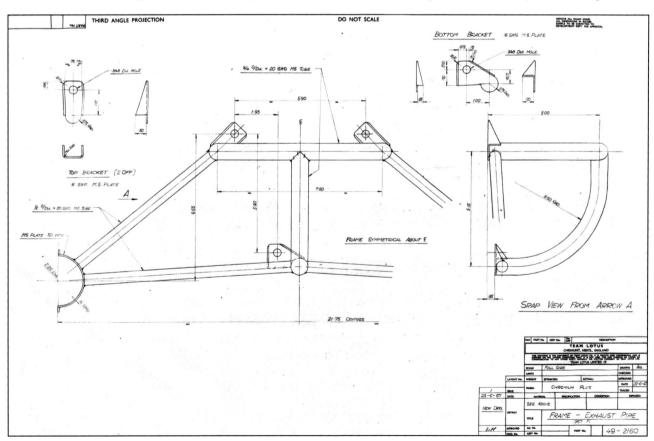

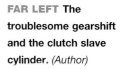

FAR LEFT The troublesome gearshift and the clutch slave cylinder. (Author)

LEFT The vulnerable gearshift mechanism. (Author)

LEFT The clutch slave cylinder. (Author)

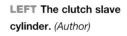

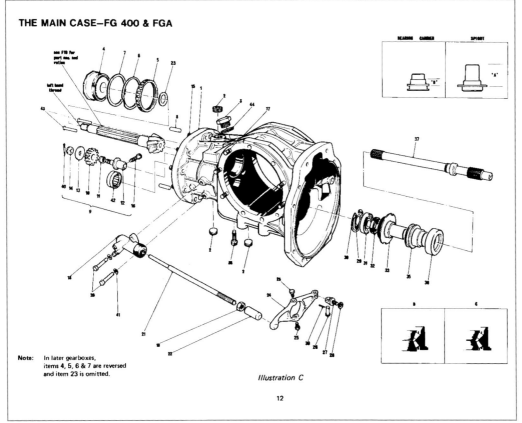

THE MAIN CASE—FG 400 & FGA

Note: In later gearboxes, items 4, 5, 6 & 7 are reversed and item 23 is omitted.

Illustration C

12

LEFT The first Hewland gearbox used in the Lotus 49 was the FG400.
(Hewland Engineering)

RIGHT The Hewland gearbox replaced the ZF in 1968. *(Author)*

RIGHT Bob Dance's notes on Hewland DG300 gearbox conversion for St Jovite.

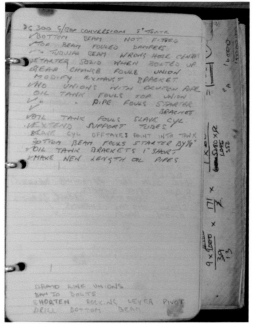

to a race, but with the advent of the DFV engine, with its abrupt torque characteristics, past knowledge was no longer much use.

Perhaps it is unsurprising that the ZF 'box only lasted one season in the Lotus 49, and

RIGHT Drive shaft on R3. *(Author)*

early in 1968 the cars appeared with the Hewland FG400 'box. Previously dismissed by Chapman, the Hewland was easy to strip down, multi-adjustable and allowed speedy changes of gear ratios. Weighing 110lb (50kg), the FG400 was a hybrid unit developed for use with the DFV and comprised an FT200 Formula 2 gear pack put on to a DG300 final-drive section. Later in the season it would be replaced by the more robust DG300 ('DG' merely stood for 'different gearbox'), which weighed 117lb (53kg). First used by Brabham to win the World Championship in 1966, the DG300 remained the norm for the rest of the 49's working life.

The clutch was a Borg & Beck 7.5in (19cm) diameter twin-plate type with a transverse operating thrust race and face cam to save space.

Towards the end of the 1967 season solid torsional shafts replaced the original BRD tubular half shafts, which were unable to flex. From the 1968 French Grand Prix, Hookes-type half-shaft joints, said to be more robust, replaced the CV-type joints that had been used earlier in the year. Drive-line loadings were considerably increased with the advent of wings in 1968 as well as the introduction of new Firestone B11-compound tyres, which removed an element of cushioning. At first heavier Mercedes-splined shafts were fitted and then a succession of stronger and stronger BRD and Hardy-Spicer joints. At the end of the season Löhr & Bromkamp 'Lobro' plunging CV joints, which accepted both the engine's torque and the extremes of suspension movement, were fitted.

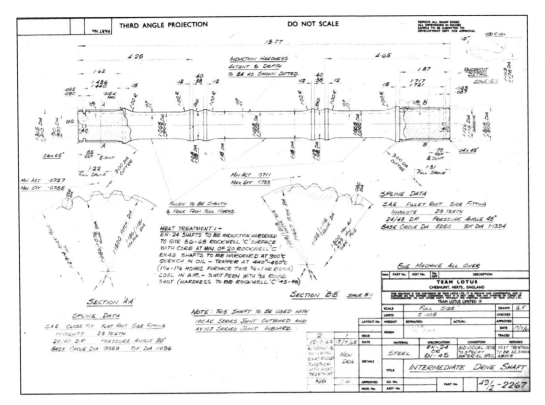

LEFT Intermediate
drive shaft drawing
from 1968.
(Classic Team Lotus)

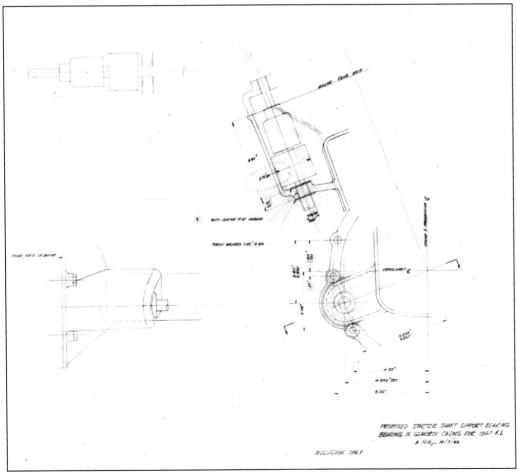

LEFT 1966 drawing
for a proposed starter
shaft support bearing
in the gearbox casing.
(Classic Team Lotus)

ABOVE The gas-turbine Lotus 56B proved to be a blind alley. It was not until 1971 that it made its grand prix début, driven by Dave Walker. (sutton-images.com)

BELOW Leo Wybrott's test of the Lotus 57/58 led to much speculation as to the identity of the driver. (Leo Wybrott collection)

SEARCH FOR A SUCCESSOR TO THE TYPE 49

There is a tendency to regard the wedge-shape, side-radiator Type 72 as the grand prix successor to the Lotus 49. As far as grand prix successes are concerned, this is true. However, this was a period of experiment and Colin Chapman sought to replace the relatively straightforward 49 with something a little more innovative. There are, in fact, three Lotus Formula 1 type numbers between 49 and 72, all of them belonging to very unconventional cars.

The Type 56 gas-turbine car, which was built to contest the Indianapolis 500, was used for a road race at Mosport in 1968 and it showed some potential, resulting in a plan – a relatively low-priority one – for a Formula 1 version, the 56B, with a Pratt & Whitney gas-turbine engine of 3-litre equivalency. The engine was not ready until 1970 and the car did not appear until 1971, when it contested three grands prix as well as some non-championship races, including the International Trophy at Silverstone, where Emerson Fittipaldi qualified it on the front row of the grid. In its final race, the Preis der Nationen, a Formula 5000 affair, Fittipaldi again

placed the car on the front row and finished second, setting fastest lap. Although the Lotus 72 did not win a grand prix in 1971, it was Lotus's established Formula 1 contender and the experimental 56B was shelved.

Chapman also proposed a Formula 1/2 car, the Type 57/58, featuring front and rear de Dion axles in the quest to keep its wide tyres in perpendicular contact with the ground. A wedge-shape prototype was tested with both a 1,600cc Cosworth FVA engine as well as a DFV, and featured a forked-pedal braking system. Jim Clark was due to try it during the week following his fatal accident and instead Graham Hill tested it, in Formula 2 format. After this test the project was abandoned as it seemed to offer no obvious advantages, only to be revived later in the year with the return of Leo Wybrott to the team to see if it could be made suitable for the Tasman series. A 2½-litre DFW engine was fitted and Wybrott carried out the initial testing at Hethel and, from his inexperienced position, thought it was quick, but Hill then took over the testing and did not like it.

'I remember Graham driving the de Dion car,' recalls Dick Scammell, 'and saying that it was absolutely fantastic and wonderful to drive – but the only trouble was that it was slow!'

As a tailpiece, a photograph of Wybrott's test duly appeared in the following day's *Daily Mail*, with the observation that this was 'Chapman's revolutionary new grand prix car.' There was much debate in the motoring press as to the identity of the driver.

The 57/58 was quietly retired to obscurity. Looking at it today, one is impressed by the fact that it preceded the Type 72 by two

years although its wedge profile, unlike that of the 72, was achieved by means of a rear-mounted radiator.

The four-wheel-drive Ferguson P99 Formula 1 car of 1961 and the subsequent use of Ferguson transmission at Indianapolis indicated the potential of four-wheel-drive technology. Chapman saw this as a way of replacing the 49, which he thought had a limited shelf life. The result was the Type 63, which had its DFV reversed in the chassis and its clutch assembly behind the driver's seat. The transmission was taken through a five-speed Lotus Hewland gearbox to a central torque-split unit on the left-hand side of the car with propeller shafts driving off-set ZF final drives on front and rear axles. Matra, McLaren and even Cosworth thought along similar lines and all produced short-lived four-wheel-drive cars that year.

The Lotus 63 was run alongside the Type 49 for some races in 1969, driven by John Miles, Mario Andretti and Jo Bonnier. A measure of how it was unloved by the team's main drivers was indicated at the British Grand Prix when Chapman tried to force them into it by creating a shortage of 49s only to have to borrow one back from a private entrant, Jo Bonnier, when they refused to drive the four-wheel-drive car. Bonnier's 'reward' was a one-off drive in a 63 that weekend.

Rindt was persuaded to race one in the Oulton Park Gold Cup, where he finished second. However, the 63 had a considerable weight penalty and general lack of feel, and with the conventional cars now getting their power down more effectively thanks to wider tyres, four-wheel-drive development was abandoned.

Chapman observed that the first time a driver went near the limit with a 63, he so terrified himself that he never went near it again. The drivers were happiest with the car when the torque split was adjusted to feed all power through the rear wheels, which made the whole thing rather pointless!

'The four-wheel-drive programme was a disaster,' recalls Dick Scammell. 'Everybody,

LEFT Leo Wybrott still has the newspaper cutting showing the mysterious test driver.

including Cosworth, thought it was the answer. We started off with a sensible front-to-rear split for a four-wheel-drive car but the only way we could make it handle was to gradually reduce the drive to the front. I remember Jochen getting out of the car and Colin asking him about it. His response was to say he was off to have a cup of tea because "you can't make it any worse". The drivers would lift off and it would flex both ends of the car. We were forced back to the 49 because it was quicker. Colin did not want to do that, but common sense prevailed.'

BELOW A Lotus 63 being refuelled at Silverstone during the 1969 British Grand Prix meeting, where McLaren and Matra also had four-wheel-drive cars; such cars would never appear again in such numbers. (Author)

RIGHT Jochen Rindt did eventually drive a Type 63, finishing second in the 1969 Oulton Park Gold Cup. (Ford)

'I found the Lotus 49 to
be phenomenal.'

Mario Andretti
Gold Leaf Team Lotus driver, 1968–69

Chapter Three

The driver's view

A total of 16 drivers qualified a Lotus 49 for World Championship grands prix. Graham Hill was easily the most prolific with 39 races in Lotus 49s, followed by privateer Jo Siffert with 22. Right from the start the package of this chassis with the Cosworth DFV engine was the envy of rival drivers.

OPPOSITE South African Grand Prix, Kyalami, 1969: two Lotus World Champions – Graham Hill (1968, Type 49) and Mario Andretti (1978, Type 79). *(Ford)*

Jim Clark's comments after the 1967 Dutch Grand Prix perhaps sum it up. Delighted with the result, he knew that the car was a winner. He understood, though, that it did not share the reliability of the Type 25 and 33 cars with which he had won his World Championships. According to Lotus historian Michael Oliver, that brought about a change in his tactics, the Scot thereafter trying to do just enough to win rather than simply crush the opposition. Perhaps he was following Juan Manuel Fangio's dictum that the best way to win a race is at the slowest possible speed and by the narrowest margin.

Clark was asked about the new Lotus 49 by David Phipps for the 1967/68 edition of *Autocourse*. He replied: 'Well, I think the first thing is that it has twice the horsepower of most Formula 1 cars I have driven before. In itself the extra power isn't really a problem, but it does have a tendency to come in with a sudden rush at about 6,500rpm and although people say the revs should not drop this low it is sometimes very difficult to avoid it with a fixed-ratio gearbox.'

Clark had a tendency to go deep into a corner with the brakes on and Phipps asked him if this was a problem with the 49: 'Yes, it feels as if the car gets up on its back wheels, and as you turn into the corner the back end tends to flick out very suddenly.'

As to whether the chassis was as good as any previous Lotus he had driven, Clark was not sure as he said it was impossible to think of the chassis separately from the engine and the 'pretty rigid' tyres. Like the Lotus 18, you were likely to be in trouble if you got out of line except when on full power.

There seems little doubt that the car was a delight to drive and all its surviving pilots are in agreement about this. All but Jackie Oliver first experienced the Lotus 49 in its later years, by which time it had been well sorted – and had become universally appreciated. It handled well, with better traction out of corners than its competitors. It was also structurally sound, which enabled its drivers to walk away from accidents that might otherwise have had more serious consequences. 'Not a bad old tool,' observed Graham Hill to camera after his first drive at Snetterton.

Peter de Klerk, the last surviving Southern African driver to have raced a Type 49, described it as 'the best car I have ever driven'.

There was a question mark about reliability and Jochen Rindt expressed his concern about this during his early races with the Type 49 'down under', but, like Clark before him, he was convinced that it was a race-winning car. Dave Sims recalls: 'Jochen loved it. He asked the Old Man if he could use a 49C at Monza in 1970 [the event at which Rindt was killed] instead of the 72.'

Jackie Oliver

In accepting a works seat following Jim Clark's fatal accident at Hockenheim, Jackie Oliver had arguably the hardest act to follow for any Formula 1 'rookie'. Colin Chapman was not happy when he turned up for his first grand prix, Monaco, with his girlfriend in tow. He then crashed on the first lap coming out of the tunnel 'avoiding someone else's accident'. It was not going to be an easy season.

'My first experiences of the Lotus 49,' recalls Oliver, 'were testing it at Snetterton and Hethel in 1967 when Jimmy and Graham weren't around. Then when Jimmy died at Hockenheim in 1968 I took over for the third grand prix of the year. I then drove it with Graham throughout the 1968 season. I have also since raced one at the Goodwood Revival.

'The first experience was at Snetterton. That was just a shakedown test. I managed to get to the end of the straightaway on the out lap

BELOW Peter de Klerk described the Lotus 49 as 'the best car I have ever driven'.
(www.motoprint.co.za)

ABOVE Called in after Jim Clark's death, Jackie Oliver had his first experience of Formula 1 in a Lotus 49. *(Bob Sparshott collection)*

ABOVE Oliver came up through the ranks of Formula 2: here on the grid at Crystal Palace he is furthest from the camera, alongside Jochen Rindt – another future Lotus 49 driver – and Jacky Ickx. *(Author)*

and, when I stuck the brakes on, a bolt didn't hold but thankfully I was going very slowly and all I did was smash the instruments with my knuckles. Testing after Zandvoort was an exercise in making sure that it did not fall apart.

'I had a lot of experience with the Lotus 48 Formula 2 car and there was much similarity. Both had an aluminium monocoque, and the Type 49 just had more power, while being bigger and heavier. Sitting in the monocoque was a difficult thing to do because you had to make a seat out of something that was not originally designed to hold a person. We didn't have seat belts in those days and the biggest problem you had was trying to keep the upper torso from flopping around. The only solution was to use shoulder pads. It was all confined. The gear lever was bent and came out from the side just underneath the steering wheel. It still had that old traditional thing that Colin did, which still amazes me, of a little wooden knob on the gear lever. There must have been something more ergonomic to do.

'When it was on a lean mixture the Cosworth engine was not the easiest thing to get off the line. Once you got it underway, the power band in what was a light, stiff chassis provided amazing acceleration and braking, which I had not experienced before. Its handling characteristics were superb. The rear suspension of the earlier cars meant that there was a bit of a problem with regard to traction. Its biggest fault then was breakaway under traction. Colin gradually managed to sort that out but I didn't get that until towards the end of the 1968 season.

'The transformation of the car came when we introduced the aerodynamic developments, which masked all the nervousness that was inherent in the car. The most unbelievable experience was at the French Grand Prix at Rouen when Colin put the high wings on the car.

'The 1968 British Grand Prix would have been a nice box to tick. You have got to be in the right car at the right time. It was the right car but the wrong time. My performance that day led to a contract with BRM. Its car was old technology with quite a powerful engine. It was dreadful getting out of the Lotus into that.

BELOW The remains of Oliver's Type 49 after his massive crash at Rouen in 1968. *(Ford)*

BRM suffered from the same reliability problems as Colin did but he was trying to push the envelope of technology, which they weren't. I complained immediately that we didn't have a modern car. Look at the Lotus 49, I said, and that was from the previous year!

'I have often wondered what happened after I left because Jochen got in the car after me and it was still a 49. Colin seemed to have got stuck in a groove but by then it wasn't good enough, even with a very quick driver.

'The 49 was successful because of what was bolted to the back and the way in which it was made. The rest of it was just an overgrown version of the Formula 2 car that I had campaigned. It was high off the ground and it was completely unaerodynamic. It was basically a round tube with suspension glued to it. It still had rocker arm suspension at the front. Mechanically, apart from the high wings that we stuck on the car, it was still old thinking

but using modern construction techniques. As a result, once someone else saw the results of sticking a Cosworth engine behind a car, the 1969 season evaded the team but with Colin, being Colin, the penny soon dropped.'

In 1999 Oliver was invited to drive David McLaughlin's recreation of a Lotus 49 in the Glover Trophy at Goodwood, a race that was won by Geoff Farmer in 49/R7. 'It was absolutely impossible to drive. It was not set up properly with regard to corner weights, toe in, toe out, and camber changes to the rear suspension. Even in third gear it would spin its wheels. We worked through it during the weekend and got it a little bit better. Goodwood can sometimes take your breath away. It really enforced the weaknesses of the 49; they were greatly exaggerated if the car was not set up properly. Its rear suspension was its Achilles heel. I did a full 360 through Fordwater with it during the race. That was a typical bend that the Lotus 49 did not like because it was a fast corner that dropped away on the exit. It could have been an expensive mistake!'

A final word from Dick Scammell: 'Jackie Oliver was reasonably easy to work with, but I think he used to argue a bit with Colin!'

Mario Andretti

Colin Chapman observed that running Mario Andretti, who put a Lotus 49 on pole for his first grand prix, was like having Jim Clark back in his team.

'It was the highest compliment that could have been paid to me,' recalled Mario. 'I met Colin at Indianapolis in 1965 when Jim won and I finished third. I said I would like to do Formula 1 some day. He said, "Mario, when you think you are ready, call me".

'I knew I needed a lot of road experience. I embarked on the Ford Le Mans programme and was at every test! I also won most of the USAC road races so, in 1968, I called Colin and said I would like to do the last two races of the season.

'Watkins Glen was my official first grand prix start although I practised at Monza. I was due to race in the Hoosier 100 the day before Monza and the organisers originally agreed to waive the regulation that said drivers could

RIGHT **Mario Andretti – the epitome of the American hero.** *(Bob Sparshott collection)*

not compete elsewhere that close to a World Championship event.

'All the practice times counted towards qualifying and when I left on the Friday for America I was quickest. When I came back I was tenth. I had got Bobby Unser a drive with BRM. Most people slipstreamed their team-mates at Monza to get a good qualifying lap but mine were not going to do that, so I brought my own guy. In the event, we never found out for sure what happened but we think Ferrari protested using the 24-hour rule and I was not allowed to start.

'People thought Watkins Glen was my home track. It was in the sense that it was close to where I lived but I had never been there before. I had quite a go against Jackie Stewart in practice and on my last lap I pulled it off. Something was obviously working. The records show how good the car was but for me it was a great introduction to Formula 1.

'I expected a really nice trophy for pole and I got a huge bottle of, like, Acqua di Selva. It was the weirdest thing I ever got. It was incredibly satisfying to get the pole for my first grand prix as I had the third car on the team and I didn't even get a fresh engine. Unfortunately the clutch started slipping in the race and put me out.

'I didn't even have a full team of mechanics. One of the half shafts was coming apart so Maurice Phillippe, the actual designer of the car, acted as a mechanic and fixed it. I thought I shouldn't really act like third "spit", after all I have the designer working on the car. It was the same in South Africa where I didn't qualify so well, but I gained several spots on the first lap. I still felt very comfortable with the car.

'I found the Lotus 49 to be phenomenal. It fitted me, it fitted my style just perfectly. It was my very first experience in a Formula 1 car. My first taste was just excellent, I felt very much at home. The agility of the car, as opposed to the agility of an Indycar on a road course, surprised me in a very positive way. It did not take me long to feel quite comfortable; it was just a matter of testing the limits. What a driver looks for in a race car is balance and response. You want a car that if you drive it to the limit it does not surprise you. If it gives you good feedback that is the quality of a well-designed car.

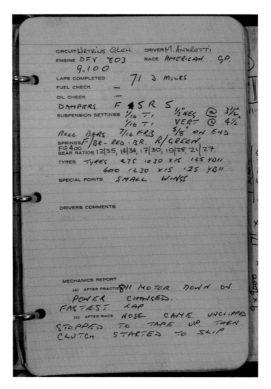

'My next Formula 1 experience was a March 701. It was like day and night: the March car was like a London bus by comparison, both aerodynamically and mechanically. A good car is a good car and among all the 196 cars that I've driven in my career the Lotus 49 goes down as a notable one. That tells you the story, it was a car that did what you told it to do.

'Certain cars, when they reach the limits, are ready to bite you back because they do not give you a clear warning. The Lotus 49 was just the opposite. It could reach the limits but it was not going to be a disaster when you went over them. Its balance was such that you could still recapture it.

'The car meant a great deal to me. Can you imagine if I had started my Formula 1 career with the March? You can't get blood out of a stone. It was a stroke of luck for me in that it was the right time. The car was well sorted out by then. Imagine the difference a good car can make to you when you're starting out on such an outing. If I had had my first outing with a lesser car it could have made a big difference in my pursuit of a Formula 1 career.

'I always got on well with Colin. I am sure that he had some reservations as to my abilities in a Formula 1 car until I demonstrated I could handle the situation and be an asset to the

A REUNION FOR ANDRETTI

ABOVE Andretti, seen with Clive Chapman and Bob Dance, was reunited with the Lotus 49 during the GP Live event at Donington. *(sutton-images.com)*

In 2007 Mario Andretti was reunited with Lotus 49 R5, long since renumbered as R10. The event, held at Donington, was a one-off celebration of Formula 1 history entitled GP Live. A small gathering watched in the pit lane on the Friday as he eased himself into the car for the first time since 1968, a wide grin on his face.

During the following day's demonstration he momentarily lost control and hit a marker, later admitting that he had completely forgotten the absence of downforce on a car of the 49's era. Getting out of the cockpit, he was heard to remark, 'I'm always keen to entertain, guys!'

team. Then he was right with me. Colin was a winner: he loved winners and I wanted to win! He gave me the equipment to do so. I could wish there had been more reliability but as far as performance is concerned the 49 was excellent. Colin had his peaks and valleys, but if you were riding with him on a peak you could get a pretty good record.'

Richard Attwood

Richard Attwood got up close and personal with Lotus 49s in the Monaco Grands Prix of 1968 and 1969. The first year, driving a usually far-from-competitive BRM P126, he challenged Graham Hill's Lotus for the lead. Twelve months later he found himself as Hill's team-mate for a one-off drive in a 49.

'I was parachuted in at the last minute after the debacle at Barcelona. Both of the regular chassis were damaged quite badly so they had to resort to chassis that were in the workshop. I don't know where they came from but they weren't the pukka number one and two cars. They were cobbled together to get to the grid for Monte Carlo. Obviously, Graham had the best one. There was no reason why he shouldn't have had! I don't know what car I had – it was just a spare hack. Jochen's car would have been quicker, for sure.

RIGHT Richard Attwood was reunited with the 49 that he drove in the Monaco Grand Prix during a Goodwood Festival of Speed press preview at Bonhams in New Bond Street, London. *(Author)*

FAR RIGHT Richard Attwood in the 1969 Monaco Grand Prix, where he finished a fine fourth. *(Bonhams)*

'I spent such a short time with the car and I can only compare it to the BRM from the year before. In that particular race I had also been parachuted in at the last minute. Both those Monaco Grands Prix were crash bang wallop, you're in the car and off you go. It wasn't the way to prepare for a grand prix. I had no idea how to condition myself to last for the 80 laps.

'The contrast between the BRM and the Lotus was quite illuminating. The BRM had basically a V12 sports car two-valve engine and it was never going to be what it needed to be. The Lotus 49 was designed for the engine and the chassis to be lightweight with a fantastic power-to-weight ratio for its period. The DFV just made it; the marriage created a fantastic car. They had gone through 1967 learning about it; by 1968 it was coming good, although it was modified later to become even better.

'Driving the BRM was like riding a horse that had just come out of a field. By comparison, the Lotus 49 was a thoroughbred. The difference between the two cars was a joke. When you touched the throttle the DFV engine just did something. The car seemed to be alive and sprightly. The response was instantaneous whether it be steering, brakes or throttle; it was a proper racing car whereas the BRM was more like a sports car. I was staggered.

'Looking back I realise that Graham Hill's win in 1968 must have been the easiest he ever had. I made the fastest race lap but that was only because Graham thought that he had done enough. He gave me a look of mutual respect but he was annoyed about that. However, it was his own fault. I remember him looking across at me at the Station Hairpin as I was closing him down, and he did a double take. There was no possibility that I could have won, but I was closer to him than he thought I should have been.

'My problem was that I did not know how to pace myself and I found at the end of the race that I had more in hand physically than I expected to have. That meant I was able to push for the last two laps but it was too late by then. Anyway, if I had increased my pace earlier Graham would simply have pulled away.

'The only real problem I had in the race was that the gear lever knob came unscrewed. There were two things I thought about: was I going to be able to finish the race holding a steel thread (I didn't think I could) and could the knob become jammed behind the pedals? I felt that I had to retrieve it and the only way I could do this was under acceleration because as soon as I braked or went into a corner I did not know where it was. I don't know how long it took me but I did find it, although I lost quite a bit of time doing so.

'I did not drive the Lotus 49 until I got to Monaco; it was such a last-minute thing. I did not know I had a drive until that week. Testing? Forget all that! We initially had wings on the car but that meant nothing to me, as I had never raced with them before. Then the CSI banned them not long after the Thursday practice sessions had finished. Graham's car had an upswept engine cover, which probably did not do much good at all. Nevertheless, Lotus had a great result with first, third and fourth, as Jo Siffert was in another 49.'

John Miles

The cerebral John Miles was the fifth and final regular Team Lotus driver to race the Lotus 49, in 1970. He had spent the previous year developing the four-wheel-drive Lotus 63 and had driven this in five grands prix. When the Type 72 proved to have a difficult gestation

ABOVE John Miles spent more time in 1969 with the Type 63 than he did the 49. *(Ford)*

BELOW Emerson Fittipaldi preparing for his maiden grand prix, at Brands Hatch in 1970. *(Ford)*

to competitiveness, Miles found himself in a 49 for the 1970 South African and Monaco Grands Prix, although he failed to qualify in Monte Carlo.

'By the time I got to the Lotus 49 it was a very well sorted car,' said Miles. 'It was reliable and nothing fell off. It was a massive contrast to the Lotus 72, even after the anti-dive and anti-lift had been taken off. I went tyre testing at Kyalami prior to the South African Grand Prix. The car was nicely balanced and easy to set up. Having gone through two seasons of racing with the previous incumbents, it did not need much adjustment. It was not a question of fiddling around with areas such as bump stops and springs – essentially it was all there.

'In South Africa I thought, "I'm beginning to make progress here", but, of course, I wasn't. It's a dangerous thing to make assumptions in motor racing. I had never been to Monaco before, not that I had previously been to Kyalami, and in those days it was a very daunting place. This was a period when graded drivers got a guaranteed start; I should have been on the grid with the time I set but I was bumped off by graded drivers. That was very disappointing. Salt was rubbed into the wound when the car was painted blue overnight and Graham Hill drove it.

'Like the 72, the Type 49 went through a series of catastrophes with suspension breakages and wings falling off. However, many components were made stronger during that period.'

A final thought from Dick Scammell: 'Poor old John got the short end of the stick.'

Emerson Fittipaldi

Like Mario Andretti, future World Champion Emerson Fittipaldi made his grand prix début in a Lotus 49.

'It was the first grand prix car I drove,' he remembered. 'It was one of the last races for the Lotus 49 and it was already fully developed. The car had already existed for three years. I raced it three times, in the British, German and Austrian Grands Prix. The one I most enjoyed was at Hockenheim. At the British Grand Prix I had problems with an exhaust pipe and the engine was misfiring a little bit; it was my first race and I was too tense. When it came to Germany I was much more relaxed, the car was performing well and I finished fourth.

'The Lotus was a great car, very easy to drive because it had great balance and was very predictable. There were no surprises. It had a lot of suspension travel and was a very soft car. It was a good car for me to start my grand prix career, a lot of fun to drive. When I then took over the Lotus 72 it was a completely different car, with a new way to drive. The 72 was much more nervous – you needed quick reactions.

'I was lucky to race the Lotus 49. With the Cosworth engine it was one of the most successful combinations in grand prix racing. I was there watching at Monte Carlo when Jochen won the 49's last grand prix. I first sat in a grand prix car when I was working at Team Lotus in Hethel at the end of 1969. Herbie Blash, who had been Jim Clark's mechanic, called me over and asked if I wanted to sit in one – it was Jochen's car.

'Colin had already invited me to race in Formula 1 at the end of 1969 but I told him that I wanted to get more experience. I only felt ready mid-season in 1970 after having done a lot of Formula 2 races. The 49 was the ideal car for me to start with.'

Tony Trimmer

On 9 April 1971 Tony Trimmer became the last person to race a factory Lotus 49, at Oulton Park in the Rothmans/*Daily Express* International Spring Trophy, which was a fairly minor affair. A former Monte Carlo Formula 3 race winner, Trimmer had already assisted with the development of the later Lotus 72, an example of which he had driven in the Race of Champions at Brands Hatch the previous month.

'It was a last-minute deal,' Trimmer recalls, 'as Lotus felt they owed me something. Everything was a rush; the car was not set up for racing. In fact, I think it may have been used as a display car. It handled atrociously. In practice, I remember taking off over Clay Hill in a straight line and landing sideways. Why did that happen? I wasn't even going that quickly.

'Peter Warr [the team manager] wasn't at all interested. He and I did not see eye-to-eye, perhaps because I had turned down another year in Formula 3 with Lotus. The mechanics were more involved with the other cars. You just don't know what you will get until you turn up. Everybody knew what a brilliant car the Lotus 49 was but I didn't enjoy the race at all. I was just fighting to stay on the track and to keep alive.'

LEFT Tony Trimmer sits in his factory Lotus 49 while Eddie Dennis and colleagues work on the car – in sophisticated surroundings! *(Tony Trimmer collection)*

'The Lotus 49 was quite straightforward to work on.'
Bob Dance
Team Lotus mechanic

Chapter Four

The mechanic's view

Colin Chapman worked his mechanics hard but they will point out that the results showed that he did things the right way. During the active life of the Lotus 49 there were regular reshuffles in the team, the chief mechanic being replaced after each season. However, there is no doubting the pride with which these loyal, dedicated men recall their time with the Lotus 49.

OPPOSITE Colin Chapman's relentless quest for improvement and innovation meant that the Team Lotus mechanics worked harder than any other crew in Formula 1. *(Ford)*

There seems little doubt that, during the 1960s, the Team Lotus mechanics worked longer hours that anyone else in the grand prix paddock – Colin Chapman was a hard taskmaster. 'Sometimes with the all-nighters it almost got to breaking point but you just had to soldier on,' says 1968 chief mechanic Bob Dance.

Despite this, there is a tremendous sense of pride among those who worked for Team Lotus in the days of the Lotus 49, a feeling of a job well done, as well as having been a part of motor racing history. As Bob Sparshott, Graham Hill's mechanic during his 1968 World Championship season, recalls, Chapman could drag the best out of them and was able to give them a grounding that would ensure successful careers for many of them once they had left the company. It is a sentiment echoed by Allan McCall, who worked on Jim Clark's car throughout 1967.

'Colin wasn't easy to work with,' says Bob Dance. 'When he was in a good mood he was fantastic and you always hoped that you could keep him happy. To be fair, we were a good team of chaps and we kept together throughout the 1968 season. We worked well together under a lot of pressure.'

The turnover of mechanics, however, was regular and there was a new chief mechanic for each of the Lotus 49's four seasons. Dick Scammell held the post in 1967. Bob Dance took over the following year as Scammell was promoted; despite being part of the championship-winning team of 1968, Dance was initially taken off the Formula 1 team for the following year, Leo Wybrott becoming chief mechanic. And as the Type 49 moved over for the Type 72 in 1970, so Gordon Huckle took on the post. There was also some lack of continuity in the rest of the team as people dropped out or were replaced.

'I suppose Colin felt that if you got new people,' surmised Dance, 'they'd all be bright-eyed and bushy-tailed, and ready to be used up!'

One third of those who worked on the Lotus 49, however, did go on to be mechanics for the Type 72. Eddie Dennis is an example: he was a mechanic on the 49, became the gearbox specialist in 1969, and then became chief mechanic for the 72.

Dick Scammell

Dick Scammell joined Lotus as a junior in 1960, rising to become Jim Clark's personal mechanic during 1962 and '63. He was chief mechanic in 1967 and involved with the Lotus 49 from the very start.

'Once the monocoque had been built,' Scammell remembers, 'it was then up to us mechanics to finish the car. Then the engine turned up and it was obvious right away that it was very powerful. Keith Duckworth had done a very good job and it was a very neat and tidy package. We started to attach the engine to the car and hang the rear suspension on it.

'We were always late. We never could keep up: the job list was always longer than you could achieve. We arrived late for the Dutch Grand Prix and got a rocket from Colin. We had just got a new transporter and it was very low-geared.

'There we had a problem with the rear hubs. Keith stood at the bench all night and filed up spacers for us. In those days you might see the designer of the engine working at a bench all night! We were all knackered at Zandvoort.

'I was quite nervous at the start. During the middle of the race it all seemed OK and then it got into the last 10 laps. Then the nervousness started to come back! We were delighted with what we did because we did not go there that well prepared. Really, it was a great relief.

TEAM LOTUS FORMULA 1 MECHANICS 1967–70

Hywel Absalom	Billy Cowe	Allan McCall	Dick Scammell
Graeme Bartels	Bob Dance	Derek Mower	Trevor Seaman
Mike 'Herbie' Blash	Eddie Dennis	Jim Murdoch	Dave 'Beaky' Sims
Dougie Bridge	Jim Endruweit	Dale Porteous	Bob Sparshott
Sid Carr	Gordon Huckle	Roger Porteous	Leo Wybrott

'One of the things Colin did for the team was that you always thought you had a car that was going to win. There was no other way of looking at it. The previous year had been my worst in motor racing but we had been told that there was something coming down the road.

'The DFV was a brilliant engine, the most powerful out there. But we had problems; we should have won the World Championship that year. The throttle system on the engine being like it was, the power curve went up to 7,000rpm reasonably steeply, then dropped around 7,500rpm and then came vertically out of a hole. So, for the driver it was a nightmare.

'We also had a problem with the gearbox, which was not up to the power that the engine was producing. The actual 'box was very good but the casing wasn't strong enough around the crown wheel and pinion, which used to take teeth off. We had drama at Le Mans and Colin announced that we were all going to Friedrichshafen [ZF's base in south-west Germany]. We packed up the trucks and drove everything there. The gearboxes were taken into the workshop and they all looked at them. They made some improvements but they were really only marginal.

'We went back to the factory after British Grand Prix practice and took all the bits that we could off Graham's crashed car and put it on the new chassis. That was one of the biggest efforts the mechanics made in one go. Then, to have that bolt come out seemed a bit unfair. It was a bad piece of the timing.

'The 49 was quite a good car to work on and it had reasonable access. When he saw mechanics struggling with something, Colin would occasionally say to Maurice Phillippe, "Why don't you do that and see how difficult it is; perhaps next time you could find a better way."

'We had learned about fireproof rubber fuel tanks by that stage; they were originally horrific to work with because they were fairly stiff. They were really aircraft tanks and there was better access on a plane. Everybody ended up with very sore, red arms.'

For 1968 Scammell became team manager, a post he retained until 1972.

'That meant I now had to look after our people and was in charge of getting it done. I now travelled a lot with Colin and got my own

LEFT **Dick Scammell in 2014.** *(Author)*

pilot's licence. I used to quite like travelling. Once you left the factory, the only thing you had to worry about was getting to the circuit through all the customs. It was light relief to be in a truck somewhere on the continent. We used to drive round the clock, often changing drivers on the move. Coming down mountain passes the driver would stand on the brake pedal and the passenger would heave on the handbrake, hoping we could stop before the next hairpin. The game in those days was to

BELOW **Dick Scammell and Colin Chapman look to the skies as Graham Hill prepares to test the prototype Lotus 49 at Snetterton.** *(Ford)*

The first person to drive a Lotus 49 was neither Jim Clark nor Graham Hill, nor even the chief mechanic, Dick Scammell. It was Mike Costin, the 'Cos' of Cosworth, who was still a Lotus employee at the time, and at Keith Duckworth's suggestion he drove it up and down the runway at Hethel. Bob Dance's 'little black book' reveals that the car's engine was DFV number 702.

Scammell takes up the story: 'He said to me, "It's a bit of a handful. You have tracked the car, haven't you?" I assured him that we had, so he drove it again and he still said it wasn't very good. Of course, we hadn't tracked the car, and he knew we hadn't. The wheels were pointing in all directions.'

Costin did indeed know: 'Dick didn't set the car up. The back wheels were pointing out two and a half inches. They were taking the piss out of me, saying I hadn't driven anything this powerful before. I said it didn't matter how powerful it was.

'The next day we went to Snetterton, where I did about 20 laps, and it all went well apart from the top radius arms failing. Maurice [Phillippe] had done a good job designing them but the load was just too much for the job, so they had to be beefed up. Dick said it was my fault for putting a wheel up on a kerb – I thought, well, it's obviously going to need to go over a bit of kerb!

'When I worked out the maximum rpm down the straight, the rolling radius and the gear ratios, I realised I had been doing 175mph at Snetterton. I should have thought about that before the hairpin! What did for the radius arm brackets was when I went round the hairpin all the joints were proud. As I was accelerating out in second and third gears there was a bit of wheelspin over the concrete.'

Scammell recalled that Hill was the next to drive the car, again at Snetterton. 'We had the top radius arm mounting fail; we had to go back and strengthen the pick-ups for the radius arms.'

Costin had another memorable encounter with the Lotus 49 two years later. 'We had new crankshafts and rods made for five engines and these were rebuilt as 2½-litre units for the Tasman series in 1969. By the end of the New Zealand leg of the series, the team was down to one serviceable engine, which was in Graham's car.'

The story of what happened next begins at a flying club near Kidderminster where Costin was visiting for the first time with his glider. He was on the runway when someone approached him from the clubhouse saying that Colin Chapman was on the phone, having tracked him down.

'It was decided that I would have to go to Australia to sort out the engine situation as I was the only person who could do everything necessary. Colin said there was a round-the-world ticket waiting for me. I went round the stores picking up all the parts I thought we would need and I took them as excess baggage. When I got there I took the heads off several engines and rebuilt one to go in Jochen's car. The outcome was that he went out and won the race. It really was a hard trip – in those days it took 39 hours to fly to Australia.'

BELOW No photographs exist of Mike Costin's drive in the Lotus 49 – but Colin Chapman was quick to get behind the wheel of his creation.
(Ford)

leave Ostend and not to lift off before you got to Brussels. Once the steering broke on the Jabbeke highway.

'Everybody thought that Lotus worked harder than everybody else and I think we did… and it showed in the results. We raced all sorts of things – we must have been mad. Think of the size of the teams now: we did everything with basically two people per car. Colin ran things in a very strict fashion. He had a little book and he wrote everything down in it. When we got back you saw him in his office and he would say, "These are the things we must do". The night before you were about to go to the next race he would check that everything had been done. He was very tidy of mind. He worked endless hours – after 6 o'clock at night he used to run Team Lotus.

'When we went to Monaco and they banned the wings, Indy was going on too. I was in charge at Monte Carlo and Colin was at Indianapolis. We thought we had to make some effort and put something on the car, if only at the back, instead of the wings. We hadn't finished this when Colin flew in for the race, so he took off his jacket and helped. After the race, returning to Nice, we drove all the way on the wrong side of the road. After a fraught flight home, he said he would see me in the office the next morning at 8:00. I was a few minutes late so he asked me where I had been and I could see from his look that he wasn't playing. We looked at the job list, then he got up, went back to his Navajo plane and flew himself back to Heathrow, parked and took a flight to Indy.'

Bob Dance

Bob Dance was chief mechanic for Team Lotus during 1968, the year when Graham Hill won the World Championship, and he describes it as 'a high-pressure season'. The statistical story of that achievement in 1968 was carefully recorded in Dance's little black book, a tome that has become almost legendary. Scammell, Dance's predecessor as chief mechanic, observed: 'Working for Colin was quite hectic so I cannot imagine how Bob had the stamina to write his diary.' Dance took up his duties as chief mechanic at the end of the

1967 season, having been on the Formula 2 team that year.

'My first job in the role was to collect the cars from Heathrow on their return from the Mexican Grand Prix. We then took them directly to Jarama for a non-championship race, with the spares still in their wooden packing cases, and loaded everything into an AEC transporter. We got to the Franco-Spanish border, which was always trouble, and got held up. It was nice weather so we unloaded and cleaned the cars, unpacked the boxes and put the spares back where they should be in the truck. After many phone calls from the Automobile Club in Madrid, we finally got clearance from customs to move on at some hideous hour of the evening. Finally we got down to Jarama, which in those days was a brand-new circuit, and had another good weekend.

'Back in the UK we prepared the cars for South Africa again for Jimmy and Graham. For that event we were still virtually the old team, with Gordon Huckle and Dougie Bridge, as the new team did not come into place until the first European race. The cars were in good shape and we had another win, but unfortunately it was Jimmy's last grand prix. We stayed to do some testing with Graham and R4 – Gordon did the first day, I did the second – while Jimmy took a night flight to New Zealand for the Tasman series. That was the last I saw of him.

'Then the 49B came on stream. Following Jimmy's death, Graham said that we had to pick ourselves up and get on with the job. We started off the European season back in Spain, at Jarama. It was a bad trip: we had the new car and we had the old one too, but just the one

ABOVE Bob Dance, seen here at Goodwood in conversation with Jim Clark's former girlfriend, Sally Swart (*née* Stokes), has continued to work with Classic Team Lotus. (*Author*)

driver, Graham. And then when we got to the border we found out that Mike Spence had been killed at Indy [in the Lotus 56 gas-turbine car].

'The Old Man was really at a low ebb and said that he would not be coming to Spain. He told Jim Endruweit, who was the racing manager, that he didn't mind what we did but we were not to run a new car. So it was left to Jim and Graham to make sure the show was on the road. Graham said, "Right lads, we've go to get on with it." He was a no-messing-about man. We did two all-nighters at Jarama. One of the mechanics, Sid Carr, blew a gasket and left about then. The night before the race we all went out to a flamenco restaurant – that was unprecedented. However, we won again, which, of course, boosted morale.

'Young Jackie Oliver then came on board as number two driver. He was really in at the deep end. We headed for Monte Carlo where Graham won, which was great for us, and Jackie blotted his copybook. Taking your lady friend with you was a bit of a "no no", particularly if you were a new driver. Before the start the Guvnor told Jackie that this was a race in which he could score points if he kept running to the end. So, keep out of trouble. First lap, he shunted. Finally, he walked back

and the Old Man went absolutely spare. Jackie copped one of his special rockets, which probably changed his approach to grand prix racing forever.

'We did two all-nighters before we left for Spa and as a result Dale Porteous and I, in the van, were the last to leave the factory and we missed first practice; we were locked out as they used to shut the roads and we could not get in the paddock. And then we built a new car at the track – loads of work.

'A classic thing happened to us at Brands Hatch. Graham knew the track inside out. He was going pretty well in the race and then suddenly he slowed down. Afterwards he told us that the handling had changed. We looked over the car and found that the front anti-roll bar was missing. The Guvnor said we could not have put one in; it was easy to change this on the Lotus 49. So we copped the flack until a man and a young lad came up to us, saying they had been at the hairpin and had brought back something that had fallen off the car – he then handed us the front anti-roll bar.

'The Lotus 49 was quite a straightforward car to work on. The original 49s had the ZF gearbox in which you could not change the ratios, only the final drive, the crown wheel and pinion. So we would go away with three built-up 'boxes per car: the one we thought would be right for the circuit, plus two others that were a ratio up and a ratio down. If the ratio was wrong, you just changed the complete package. That was quite straightforward, although it threw a lot of work on the gearbox department people; we used to have a gearbox man travelling with us. Then we moved on to Hewland gearboxes with the 49B and they were OK. We also got involved in development of constant-velocity driveshafts on the 49B and with that came some unreliability.

'Later in the 1968 season, with the championship a possibility, we began to wonder about improving the reliability of the gearboxes. We had to fit a kit in Canada to provide Graham with a stronger gearbox. We were working all night in a tent in the pouring rain and it didn't all fit together – that was a saga. We also had drama in Canada with the top engine mountings, which had broken where the car had been damaged earlier on. Graham pulled in during the race, commenting that the car felt as if it had a hinge in it. We couldn't immediately see anything wrong so he continued – and scored some points – but afterwards we found that only the two bottom mountings were holding the engine on. It was dramatic stuff.

'Another major problem was the way the Guvnor wanted us to do fuel checks. The car had a seat tank, two forward side tanks with taps so you could hold the fuel in them, and yet another aluminium tank further forward, in front of the master cylinders and behind the radiator. We needed that much capacity for races like Monza and Watkins Glen. It really used to annoy Colin if we didn't get it right. He would point out that a gallon of fuel weighed seven pounds and would say, "We spend thousands getting the weight down and you lads go and stick in another gallon".'

Despite winning the World Championship, there was friction at Team Lotus. Dance believes that Chapman was 'a bit fed up with us by Monza'. He decided to appoint Leo Wybrott as chief mechanic, giving Dance the choice of transferring to the road-car side or the imminent four-wheel-drive project. Dance chose the latter, which included both the Indy effort and Formula 1.

Bob Sparshott

Bob Sparshott had been with Bob Dance in the Lotus Cortina and Formula 2 crews, and the two already had a rapport, Sparshott saying of Dance, 'He was my mentor – I aspired to be as good as him.' As Sparshott had worked on Graham Hill's car in Formula 2, it was logical that the 23-year-old should remain with Hill when he moved up to the Formula 1 squad for 1968.

'I went to the Tasman series at the beginning of 1968. I just did the four races in Australia because Graham had fallen out with the organisers in New Zealand. It was a monster trip. I got out of the plane in Sydney wearing a suit and it was very hot. Jimmy Clark met me and said we were going for breakfast. An idiot drove out in front of us on the dual carriageway so close that I nearly died but Jimmy hardly seemed to notice and kept on talking.

'We basically had a ball because there was

no management – Chapman did not go down there. Besides me, it was just Leo Wybrott and the two Porteous brothers, Dale being a full-time member with Roger co-opted in as a helper. The luck was that we had very little trouble with the cars. I don't think we changed the engine at all on Graham's car. It was good fun. The Australians took us on board.

'The one epic thing I remember was when we were given courtesy Ford four-wheel-drive vehicles to tow open trailers with the cars on. We started at Surfers Paradise. It all went surprisingly smoothly. I remember thinking – is this what it's normally like? I was driving down the Pacific Coast Highway with Leo sitting next to me, and Dale was driving the vehicle in front. It was all very picturesque. We were on a downhill bit when Dale braked rather suddenly and caught me by surprise. I over-braked and the next thing I remember was seeing the trailer out of the corner of my eye coming round alongside the 4x4 and then batting us over the edge of the road. When we stopped, the whole thing was so precarious

ABOVE We are not amused. It is 10pm and (from left) Bob Sparshott, Trevor Seaman and Bob Dance learn from Colin Chapman that they will have to stay on for an all-nighter. Maurice Phillippe (far right) will stay on with them. *(Bob Sparshott collection)*

LEFT Bob Sparshott today. *(Author)*

RIGHT Bob Sparshott
was entrusted to take
the Lotus 49 out on to
the track.
(Bob Sparshott)

BELOW Graham Hill
makes sure that Eddie
Dennis (left) and Bob
Sparshott are making
adjustments just as
he wants them. *(Bob
Sparshott collection)*

that Leo and I sat there worried about moving: the trailer was sitting on the edge of the road but without axle or wheels; the Lotus 49 was intact and didn't have a scratch; and the tow hook was preventing the 4x4 from rolling over. After a bit we realised it was probably stable enough for us to get out, and then a massive lorry with a winch came along and was able to tow us out. Somehow we managed to get the axle back on the trailer and the 4x4 was driveable, although it had dents all over it.

'When we went to Monaco, the Old Man arrived at a point when we were looking as if we had finished for the day. He came in with a stern expression, got hold of Bob [Dance] and told him to get a foolscap pad as he wanted another look at the 49B and its wedge tail. We ended up with pages of things to do and he wanted them done before the next day. I got very annoyed. He said that he and I ought to go out the back where there was a little balcony, and there he put his arm round me like a father and asked me what the problem was – within five minutes he had got me round. And, of course, we won the race. After the race, the driveshafts from the new cars were required for an Indy car. We worked on this until almost midnight. I was so shattered I just collapsed into bed. Just my luck, for I was supposed to receive the mechanic's trophy at the Café de Paris; in my place Dale Porteous took the honours and all the glamour.

'There are other odd things I remember. When Graham crashed during the Dutch Grand Prix at the Tarzan hairpin, where he locked the brakes, the car's nose ended up under the wire and there was this bloke there trying to get the leaves out of it with his umbrella. I shouted at him, but I was the other side of the wire and couldn't do anything.

'During practice for the Belgian Grand Prix, Jackie Oliver wanted to get out just after Graham. I was behind Graham's car, easing it forward so that he could engage first gear, when I got hit on the back of my legs by Jackie's car – he was a bit too anxious. I went up to his cockpit and got hold of him – I didn't think he would do it again…

'The French Grand Prix at Rouen was another huge saga. The first bit of news we got was that Dick Scammell had replaced Jim Endruweit as team manager. Then Graham turned up all bright and asking the usual questions. "Robert," he would ask [Sparshott imitates Hill's slight lisp], "have you got the set-up sheet?" He would start going through it, talking it through with his wife Bette and looking at his own notebook. In the end you'd be changing quite a few things before you turned a wheel, and you couldn't rely on anywhere in the paddock being flat so you lost the corner weights immediately. It used to annoy me. Sometimes you would go round in a full circle.

'When practice began, we could see from the pits Oliver coming out of the hairpin. He hit a gatepost, luckily on the engine mounting. We ran up the inside of the track. The car was in two bits but he had got out of the monocoque, shaking and white as a sheet. In a clever move, the Old Man told all the other teams that the bellhousing had broken, so everyone had better check theirs because we all ran the same spacer [Bob Dance, in fact, believes that Chapman was quite genuine in his concern on this point].

'Then there was the bump-stop saga at Oulton Park [about 20 minutes before the race Hill asked Sparshott to cut away a section of the rear aeon rubbers]. When the Old Man found out, he was very annoyed. Even Graham got a rocket, and we all got a big talking to after the race. "I design the cars," he said. "They are my cars. I say what is changed. If a driver wants something changed, he must come and ask me." This was before the days when a car would have its own engineer; your only source of information was the driver.'

The mechanics were not too amused when Team Lotus ran a third car, and Sparshott recalls the Canadian Grand Prix when Bill Brack was the paying driver.

'What we absolutely didn't need was a third car. Brack retired in Canada with broken driveshafts – surprise, surprise. Then just before things kicked off at Watkins Glen the news was broken to us, at about 9.00pm, that we were running Mario Andretti. Chapman wanted three changes of engine and all the constant-velocity joints rebuilt [a huge job that Bob Dance carried out], and we were also instructed to change the front springs on Oliver's car. Trevor Seaman went off sick that night and Maurice Phillippe volunteered to help. We decided to leave Oliver's springs to last. On top of all that stronger, heavier wheels also turned up the next morning.'

The next morning Dance led the mechanics out to get something for breakfast at one of the stalls around the circuit and while they were absent everyone else turned up. The first words Jackie Oliver said were, 'Colin, they haven't changed my springs.' Chapman could see that Dance was wound up and told Oliver that he had changed his mind and these were

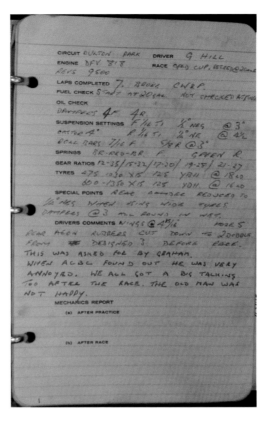

the springs that he wanted him to use. Hill was more understanding and asked the weary mechanics what he could do to help. Sparshott asked if he would be good enough to polish the car, which he got on and did. Chapman then noticed that the new wheels had not been unpacked. Sure enough, Oliver crashed when his old-style rear wheel broke. 'It was comedy, but serious,' Sparshott recalls.

'The final race of the season was a full-pressure situation. We came back to England and then went back out to Mexico. Chapman had another new idea: "I want to tape over all the rivet lines on the high wings to reduce the surface drag." There was an extra pedal to feather the rear wing and there were two bungee straps to return it to the normal position – and one of these bungees let go in the race. Again, despite the fact we were under pressure, we had a third driver, Moises Solana.'

Sparshott reckons that, by the end of the season, he had spoken out too much, although Dance thinks he is being unfair on himself. He felt he needed to move on and left to start his own business, eventually running his own Formula 1 cars.

Leo Wybrott

Having served an apprenticeship in a Vauxhall dealership in Hastings, New Zealand, Leo Wybrott made the trip to England in March 1964 and got a job in a fairly responsible position – 'a New Zealand apprenticeship teaches you everything' – with the Vauxhall dealership Shaw & Kilburn. Before long he spotted an advertisement for a travelling gearbox mechanic for a Formula 1 team, which he discovered was Team Lotus.

'At that time I had no idea how Formula 1 gearboxes worked. I remember being asked at the interview who the World Champion was. I

RIGHT Leo Wybrott (left) and Roger Porteous 'down under' for the Tasman series. *(Leo Wybrott collection)*

had no idea.' It was the travelling that interested him. He heard nothing for a while but then Jim Endruweit asked if he would start the job as soon as possible and two weeks later he was on his way to Zeltweg for the Austrian Grand Prix. His first night at the track was an all-nighter on his own changing the crown wheel and pinion in Jim Clark's ZF gearbox – 'a steep learning curve'.

Wybrott gradually moved to the position of a more general mechanic and, as a New Zealander, tended to find himself on the team for the Tasman series. It was on his return from Tasman duty early in 1967 that he found the Lotus 49 starting to take shape. He became heavily involved in the construction of the car: 'I was starting to do what I had always wanted to, have a role in a production project, building and working on the cars in the shop.' This ambition, however, was not fully realised until he left Team Lotus to join McLaren; and during 1967 he was not involved with the 49s at the track.

'While the team was at the Dutch Grand Prix we were busy building R3 and this was reasonably well advanced, to the stage of a painted monocoque with brake pipes installed, by the time of the British Grand Prix. Then Graham Hill hit the pit wall and suddenly we had to complete R3 overnight. There are lots of stories surrounding getting the car to the circuit the following morning, race day, getting lost and having to drive through the queues of cars.'

At the end of 1967 Wybrott was again asked to do the Tasman series. 'I shipped off to New Zealand with the car on my own. It went out as just a monocoque, just a kit, and I assembled it in a Ford workshop in Auckland with Roger Porteous, Dale's younger brother, who became part of the team; Dale then arrived from the South African Grand Prix with Jimmy [Clark].

'Normally the only communication with England was my regular call to Andrew Ferguson after a race. However, when we got to Christchurch there were all these panicky phone calls about the new Gold Leaf sponsorship. They were flying the paint, the gold leaf and the colour scheme out to us. We found a paint shop and worked all night painting the car; we put two little, hand-painted kiwis just behind the nose.

Within a few weeks of Wybrott's return to

England came the dreadful news that Clark had been killed. 'I had done three Tasman series with Jimmy and had become very close to him during the last one. He had been talking about his future and I think this sponsorship thing had put him off. He was thinking of starting his own company to hire out piloted aeroplanes and had asked me if I would be interested in being involved.'

Shortly after his return to the UK, Wybrott got married and he and his new wife Sarah went to France to start a new life, but it did not work out there. When they got back to England, Leo returned to work at Team Lotus, initially on the wedge-shape Type 57/58 with de Dion suspension (see Chapter Two).

For the 1969 season Wybrott joined the Formula 1 team as chief mechanic, the third man in that post since the advent of the Type 49. Only years later did he learn just how many head-to-head confrontations his predecessors, Dick Scammell in 1967 and Bob Dance in 1968, had had with Chapman. He accepted the new post on the understanding that Dance had already been told about the change, but in the event Dance only found out when the announcement was made to the team. 'Bob was very good about it and continued to help the Formula 1 team on occasion, particularly when we ran the four-wheel-drive cars.

'It was a fiasco in Barcelona. We made at least two extensions to the wings and the cars went faster, but there was no thought about what was happening in the middle of the wing. The cars were both so badly damaged, like two pieces of scrap, that we just put them in the transporter one on top of the other. Back at the factory when we hoisted the first one, Jochen's, out of the transporter, it was like a banana.

'Using one of the Tasman cars, Team Lotus was able to get two 49s to Monaco for Hill and Attwood. Then they banned the wings and we ended up doing an all-nighter to make a tray-type tail for Graham's car using panels from storage areas inside the transporter.

'Amid all this we were expected to build up the four-wheel-drive cars. There were spells that year when we hardly ever went home. We had four cars running at the British Grand Prix. We had everybody there that we could muster, including three of the team's four chief mechanics.

'At one point morale in the team became very low. The only respite came when you got into the transporter to drive to a race. We were owed prize money and the mechanics were bitching and moaning to me. When I mentioned this to Colin he went straight to the accounts department, asked the chief accountant for the cashbox, took out however many hundreds of pounds were required, came back to the shop and put the cash on my desk. We kept going and ended up winning at Watkins Glen, where 10 per cent of the prize money was paid to us after the race in dollars – I duly took this back to our hotel and counted it all out.'

A particular incident, known as 'the golden rivet affair', stands out in Wybrott's mind: 'On one occasion, when a fuel bag was pulled out, a mechanic discovered that a rivet had not been dollied properly and had chafed through the bag. When Colin found out he went absolutely berserk. He was holding the rivet and gave it back to me during his lecture. I just threw it over my shoulder – which set him off again.

'At Monza we had a misfire on Jochen's car. We thought we had fixed it but we couldn't be sure because we couldn't try it after practice. So it was arranged that we would get to the track very early the next morning and I would try out the car on part of the circuit. When we were due to leave the hotel it was pouring with rain so I told the guys they could have another half-hour in bed – sleep was vital in those days. When we did make our way to the circuit, still at a reasonably early time, the roads became drier and when we arrived we found that there hadn't been any rain at all! Dick Scammell was already there and he was furious. That was probably a very black mark for me, but it was for the right reasons.

'By the end of the season I wanted to stop racing and instead get together a group of people who could stay behind and build the cars. But during December we were all called into Chapman's office in turn, starting with me. The story was that there was a 40 per cent cut in our motor racing budget and there was no place for me. I was offered a job on the Elan assembly line. It was the same for a number of the others. The story appeared in *Motoring News*. Bruce McLaren read the article and got on the phone – and that's where I went.'

During his time as chief mechanic Wybrott's duties included driving Lotus 49s on the track at

Hethel, the former airfield where Lotus relocated in 1966, to check them out before they were sent to races, so that any problems could be fixed. It was all done properly: Wybrott had to have a medical and was always properly attired with race suit and helmet.

'You would take the car up to maximum rpm, which in those days was to 9,500, 9,600, maybe even 10,000. The more I got into it, the better I was able to drive and I became a little bit faster, although I wouldn't be lapping anywhere near a serious time. You'd be looking for anything untoward, whether an oil leak or a brake problem; when these cars were rebuilt or reassembled they were worked on by quite tired people and problems could occur.

'Late one evening with the four-wheel-drive Type 63 my goggles started to mist up and I thought it was time to stop. As I braked at the end of the straight, the right rear wheel came loose and the nut came off. I was launched into the air and mowed down a whole load of little trees...'

Allan McCall

Allan McCall was another of the many New Zealanders who found themselves working with British motor racing teams. A chance meeting with a couple of car dealers on the boat from New Zealand led him to contact Lotus when he arrived in England, with the result that he joined Bob Dance in the Lotus Cortina team before moving on to work on the 1966 Indianapolis car and then becoming Jim

Clark's mechanic for the 1967 season. In that role he was at the Lotus 49's first race – the Dutch Grand Prix at Zandvoort.

'In practice we had problems with the rear axle shafts moving in the bearings so parts had to be made up to fix this. We were working in a dark little place in town. There was a big workload on Graham's car too, so I was given two new assistants to help me through the night. These assistants were Keith Duckworth and Henry Manney, the American journalist – what a great night's entertainment that was. Jimmy went on to win and after the race I retrieved the ribbons from the laurels, which had been put on the car after the presentation. I rolled them up and put them in my toolbox and forgot about them. At a later stage I found them and still have them to this day.

'At the British Grand Prix at Silverstone, Graham crashed his car in practice so everyone returned to the factory and built up a new one for him overnight. That is everyone but me. Jim Endruweit towed me in R2 behind a red Cortina to a Ford garage in Brackley and then left me there overnight, alone, to prep the car and reinforce the radius rod brackets with what I could find lying around. The next morning I seemed to be waiting forever until Jim returned to tow the car and me back to the circuit. The traffic was terrible and half the time we were ploughing down the grass verges to make it. We arrived with just enough time to fuel up the car and do final prep for the race.

'It seems that everyone else, in their moment of glory of building up the new car overnight and rushing back to Silverstone to receive well-earned adulation, had totally forgotten about me and R2 down in Brackley. Jim had to fight his way out of the circuit through the incoming traffic to get me. I often wonder why this story never seems to be told – it was quite significant as R2 was the winning car.

'During the Italian Grand Prix Jimmy got a puncture in the right rear tyre. To change the wheel I had a large hand spanner. Someone jacked the rear while I got the wheel off. I turned to get the new wheel, but Dick Scammell, in the pit, had trouble passing it to me because of people sitting on the pit counter. I cleared the way with a big swipe along their shins with the wheel spanner and we got Jimmy away. He

was a lap down and drove an incredible race to lead again, only to run out of fuel on the last lap.

'After practice Mr Chapman had decided that we did not need much fuel to do this race and told me to put in only 31 gallons. Dick Scammell took me to one side and told me to put in 33 gallons as he reckoned the Old Man had got it wrong. I reckoned they were both wrong, so I put in 35 gallons. When questioned by Chapman after the race, I told him that I had put in extra fuel – and he said he would sack me if I ever disobeyed him again. Just think, we could have run out at least seven laps before the end of the race.

'When Jimmy won the US Grand Prix he did so with the back wheel leaning over due to a broken top rear link brace. We called these braces "pine trees" and they broke or pulled bolts on a regular basis. Mr Chapman insisted that they were strong enough and that we were fitting them wrongly or welding them wrongly.

'In Mexico, Jimmy drove the spare car, R1, as it had a fresh motor. My car, R2, was driven by Moises Solana, who did a good job running up front until the motor expired, from having too many miles on it. The official reason given, I believe, was suspension failure. This was my last race with Team Lotus.

'Working under Mr Chapman was probably the best motor racing education anyone could have. He taught you that all things were possible if you tried. He used to say, "Can't? What do you mean, can't? You mean won't." While you worked for him, I believe he was loyal to you and you could do little wrong if you were one of his lads. But when I left he never so much as said "hello" or recognised my existence. Almost all the people who had the Lotus experience went on to make their mark in the sport and I'm sure that all would agree that Mr Chapman and Team Lotus were the backbone of their careers.'

Derek Mower

Derek Mower was part of Team Lotus's Indianapolis operation in 1969. During 'the month of May' at Indy there were no Indy cars at Hethel to work on but plenty for the overstretched Formula 1 squad to do, so he was drafted in to work on its spare car, bringing him back into contact with Mario Andretti, who that year practised a works Lotus at Indy – but did not race it – and had three Formula 1 outings with Team Lotus.

'The Lotus 49 was a nice, compact, little car. There was nothing revolutionary about it. When we moved on to the Type 72, we could see how easy it had been to work with.

'With "Beaky" Sims, I took Emerson Fittipaldi to Silverstone for his first test in the car, and Jochen Rindt also came along. Emerson was obviously very quick from the start: Jochen was encouraging him to go even faster while the Old Man was trying to slow him down.'

In January 1971, Mower and Sims were the mechanics when Team Lotus ran Emerson's elder brother, Wilson, in a non-championship race in Argentina, a precursor to a World Championship race there the following year. It was arranged that Emerson would then demonstrate the car during a Formula 3 event at Interlagos, Brazil, the first time a modern grand prix car had been run there.

'We had to take the 49 from Buenos Aires to Brazil in an Air Varig Douglas DC-3 freighter. On board there were also several thousand pounds' worth of peaches in crates, and loads of fruit flies. When we took off, the crew were all wandering around, one of them drinking a beer – there was no discipline. Then there were big storms: it was really rough and the plane was bouncing all over the place, all the way to Montevideo, where we landed to refuel. There was guerilla action going on in Uruguay at the time and we weren't allowed to talk to anyone when we got out. When we set off again there was more turbulence and the cases all broke loose. The peaches ended up all over the 49 – in it, over it, everywhere. When we finally arrived at the track, after a night with no sleep, we spent hours cleaning up the car before it had to run that day.

'Emerson was determined to set an outright lap record. The Lotus 49 used to run really low at the front under braking and, if the driver wasn't careful, he could grind off the bottom of the radiator. Emerson was showing off to everyone and so intent on his quick lap that he put a hole in the radiator and totally roasted the engine. Colin Chapman had a bit of a problem with that… it was probably our fault!

Tony Cleverly's father, who had often gone to Brooklands, decided that his son would be a mechanic and that was that. In the mid-1950s Tony went to work in Rob Walker's garage. Within a few months he had transferred to the racing team. As a 'lad doing the cleaning' he was not present when Walker became the first genuine independent to win a World Championship grand prix – Argentina in 1958 – but he was present at all the subsequent victories. During much of this period the mechanics were led by the legendary Alf Francis, and after Francis's departure Cleverly took over as chief mechanic.

When Jo Siffert joined the team he brought with him Heini Mader and his friend Jean-Pierre Oberson to work on his car. During the Swiss driver's early period with Rob Walker, the team tended to run two cars, with Cleverly the mechanic on the second. However, in 1966, Siffert became the sole driver and the three mechanics worked together on his car, a Cooper-Maserati T81, for the first two years of the 3-litre formula.

'We called that car the *Torrey Canyon* as it had so much oil coming out of it all the time,' recalls Cleverly, making reference to the tanker that was shipwrecked in 1967 off the coast of Cornwall. 'It was a nightmare of a car and a relief when we got the Lotus 49. We went up to Hethel to prepare it before we took it back down to our base in Dorking.'

'After Jo knocked a corner off it at Brands, we took the car back to the workshop. We started to strip it out and that was when the fire took place. It was a spark from a drill that caused it. I ended up jumping out of the office window to get out of the place, almost ending up in the millpond. It went up like a tinderbox. There were three of us in the workshop but the other two got out of the door in time. I was on the phone trying to get the police and the fire brigade and was almost trapped. None of us were hurt, thank God.'

The Lotus 49 was destroyed, along with the Cooper-Maserati. Walker's racing records and mementoes were all lost as well, including the threadbare tyres with which Moss had finished the 1958 Argentine Grand Prix.

'I don't think Mr Walker knew what to do after the fire. Jack Durlacher [by that stage his partner in the team] and Mr Joliffe, who was the manager, told him he just had to get on with it with another car.

'We spent some time back at Hethel building the new car and arrived at Brands Hatch just in time for practice for the British Grand Prix, having been working on it all night. The bump steer on it was really way out and after the race it went back to the factory to have the steering rack remounted. It seemed impossible that we had won the race. Then we went to the next race and the car wasn't any good!

'Once we had won the race I sent the two

BELOW Tony Cleverly was Rob Walker's chief mechanic during the time of the Lotus 49. *(Tony Cleverly collection)*

BELOW RIGHT Jo Siffert tells chief mechanic Tony Cleverly how to drive the Lotus 49. *(Tony Cleverly collection)*

ABOVE Tony Cleverly (left) with Mike 'Herbie' **Blash.** *(Tony Cleverly collection)*

lads, Heini and Jean-Pierre, to go round the circuit on the winner's trailer. I stayed in the pits to look after the tools, then went back home and had a few drinks. It didn't really mean that much to me at the time, having been with Rob Walker when Stirling was winning races for him. It was not a matter of being blasé but we had won so many important races with Stirling and Alf. With Alf, you weren't allowed to get excited: you just accepted it and got on with your job of loading up the truck.

'The Lotus 49 was a great car to work on compared with the Cooper-Maserati. It was simplicity in itself. With the engine bolted to the monocoque, it was so much easier – in fact it has to be the easiest car I worked on. The Lotus 72, with its torsion bar suspension, could be a nightmare at times.

'Jo wasn't very good at setting up cars. He used to drive as quickly as he could and that was it. Things like shock absorbers and tyres make so much difference and the drivers in those days weren't into this as much as they are now.'

Cleverly left the team to start up a crash-repair business near Dorking when Rob Walker joined up with John Surtees to run the Team Surtees cars.

'Peter Warr [team manager] joined us in Brazil. "Beaky" and I had no visas and we were not allowed to leave the country after the demonstration run – and we had no money. Peter had to spend a couple of days rushing around, getting the visas sorted out.

'I remember going to Emerson's family house during that trip. Wilson was there with his new-born son, Christian. When I engineered for Keith Wiggins in Formula 3000 many years later, Christian drove for us.'

Dave Sims

Dave 'Beaky' Sims joined Team Lotus to work on Lotus Cortinas and in Formula 2 and he was employed as Jim Clark's mechanic that fateful day at Hockenheim. Unsure of his future, he asked Chapman on his return what he should do. To his surprise, the boss said he wanted him immediately to go out to the Spanish Grand Prix to help Bob Sparshott on Graham Hill's Lotus 49. For the rest of the year he worked on Jackie Oliver's car, transferring to John Miles for the 1969 Formula 1 season, during which he also worked on the build of the four-wheel-drive Type 63.

'The Lotus 49 was a very practical and straightforward car to work on. There were no massive complications. It was good to set up and pretty simple by comparison with what was to come. The Old Man did try a number of different variations though. It was typical of him that he would get an idea at the track and try that out there and then.'

Changes to the high wings at Barcelona, where Sims was working on both cars, provide an example of Chapman's improvisation. 'He said he wanted the wings to be six inches wider, so that's what we did. Jackie Stewart came up to me and asked what I was doing and said, "Have you tested this yet?"

'It created so much downforce that the wing on Graham's car collapsed in the middle. Billy Cowe and I ran out to the accident, and when we saw it Billy told me to get back to Colin as quickly as possible and tell him to bring Jochen in. I started to run but the next thing I heard was a massive crash and exactly the same thing had happened to Jochen. After the race, Stewart told Jochen, "We've got to get the FIA to clamp down on this."

ABOVE Some of the Lotus mechanics rose through the ranks of Formula 2 before working on the grand prix cars. Together in front of Oliver, Clark and Hill at Albi are (from left) Sid Carr, Dave Simms, Eddie Dennis, Ian Campbell, Bob Sparshott and Bob Dance. *(Bob Sparshott collection)*

BELOW Helicopter pilot Roger Porteous (left) was not a Team Lotus mechanic but helped out his brother Dale (right, partially obscured) and Leo Wybrott in the 1968 Tasman series. *(Ferret Fotographics)*

A memory of Chapman's ingenuity concerns that year's German Grand Prix at the Nürburgring, where Team Lotus had taken three cars. Oil-surge problems manifested themselves, which meant that the mechanics had to cut open the tanks overnight and fit baffles to stop the resulting starvation to the engine. 'The Old Man was great at getting over that sort of stuff.'

Sims was at Watkins Glen when Mario Andretti had his first race in a Lotus 49, with a chassis that had previously been used by Hill. The American, who was rather shorter than Hill, could not reach the pedals but was happy with

the solution offered by Sims and Dale Porteous: they put blocks on the pedals and stuffed a brown workshop coat behind the seat. 'We had never come across such a laid-back attitude.'

Like Mower, Sims has memories of the DC-3 flight from Argentina to Brazil, although he is convinced that the plane was full of oranges, not peaches. 'We were told that there was this young driver who was going to demonstrate the car during a Formula 3 meeting at Interlagos. We were told to be careful as we had no visas and what we were doing was not legal. However, we would be met at the airport by a trailer. When we refuelled at Montevideo we could see oil leaking out of the filthy plane's engine and the pilots were drinking cognac from their hip flasks. When we got back to England with the blown engine, Chapman said, "What the hell did you think you were doing?" But we had no pit board and certainly no radio, so we could not stop Emerson.'

Dale Porteous

Dale Porteous, who worked on Graham Hill's car during the 1967 season along with Dougie Bridge, remembers the Lotus 49 as being 'a good car to work on'. However, there was one problem that still sticks in his mind: 'To work on the balance bars you had to lie on your back.' It seems that this was usually a job for Allan McCall.

With his brother, Roger, Dale was one of those involved in fitting the 'helicopter' Tasman wing, as recorded in Chapter Two. 'It was Jimmy's idea but he wouldn't drive with it. I think he was a bit worried about what Mr Chapman would say.'

Another of Porteous's abiding memories is of Jackie Oliver's crash at Rouen in 1968. 'There's a photo of me looking at the wreck. They put it down to aerodynamics. At least that is what we were told.' Added Dave Sims, 'Jackie blamed everything under the sun, but there was no television then.'

Maintaining the Lotus 49

For this section of the book, explaining how the factory Lotus 49s were maintained and serviced, the author is indebted to Bob

Sparshott, Graham Hill's mechanic during his World Championship-winning year of 1968, for his recollections.

Following a European grand prix, the Team Lotus mechanics would have travelled back to Hethel in the transporter. Whatever time they got back – day or night, it did not matter – the engines were removed from the cars straight away, as the priority was to get them back to Cosworth for overhaul. After the DFV became widely available, it would be a race between the teams to get their engines back to Cosworth before anyone else.

Once the engines had been removed, the mechanics could then go home for a much-needed sleep while someone drove the engines to Cosworth. Depending upon the time they arrived back, this driver could be someone from the stores or one of the mechanics themselves. The following day the mechanics would return to strip out the car itself. If a car had been little used at a grand prix, its engine might be retained for another race but would still be removed and stripped of items such as the exhaust and clutch.

Each car had a crew of two. Bob Sparshott's partner in 1968 was Trevor Seaman, who was something of a gearbox specialist – so his next job would be to strip the 'box and, if necessary, change the crown wheel and pinion. The gearbox would then be rebuilt ready for the next race. When the Hewland 'box was in use, Seaman would have been informed which ratios to use.

Meanwhile, the other mechanic, Sparshott, would be working on the chassis, starting from the front. The front suspension would be taken apart and the cast uprights crack-checked with spray penetrant. There was no 'lifeing' programme so the changing of components such as wheel bearings was left entirely to the race mechanic's judgement. 'It could be argued,' says Sparshott, 'that the right thing to do would have been to put in new bearings after every race, but in those days there was a budget consideration and we weren't allowed to spend money willy-nilly. It was a judgement call, and down to us.'

The brakes would come next, with calipers checked and resealed as necessary. The steering rack would be checked for play in the outer

ABOVE **Brake calipers would be checked between races.** *(Author)*

bearings, with excessive play requiring the rack to be taken apart and new bearings fitted. The backlash on the pinion of the steering rack would also be examined and adjusted as necessary. The universal joint on the lower end of the steering column would be checked for play.

As the car understandably had to endure vibration, it was important to examine the wiring, particularly all the connections behind the dash panel. Sparshott recalls that there was always concern over the Rotax switches: these were aircraft switches of very good quality but they did occasionally fail due to vibration.

The play on the pedal bearings – the 49 used pendant pedals – was checked where they pivoted. If the pedals had to be removed, the mechanic had to be careful to take accurate measurements, such as the exact height of the

BELOW **Master cylinders would be regularly overhauled.** *(Andy Brown)*

brake pedal from the floor and the relationship of the brake pedal to the clutch and throttle. Sparshott recalls that Graham Hill could detect a difference of only a couple of millimetres.

The master cylinders were regularly overhauled to make sure that there were no seal leakages. There were two reservoirs for the brakes and one for the clutch.

The throttle cable was a heavy-duty push/pull type, of about 3mm thickness, which could be moved either way by the driver. Its condition and movement had to be checked, as there were occasions when the throttle did not close, particularly at Zandvoort where sand could get in.

Temperature gauges had to be changed regularly because of vibration. Sparshott: 'This was something of a nightmare, particularly the oil temperature gauge, because of the length of the connection back to the engine – not a job you wanted to do at a track.'

If there was no major work to be done on the chassis, in other words if there had been no accident, it would be given only a superficial look-over. There would be a crack check around the engine mountings. There was usually no need to remove the fuel tanks but sometimes the seat tank would be examined – through the hatch behind the driver's back – to ensure that there was no debris inside. Sparshott: 'Another thing you didn't want to be doing at a track.'

In the earlier part of 1968 half shafts with universal joints were used, with a sliding spline with rollers – without these the half shaft would have jammed under acceleration. Sparshott: 'The half shafts were heavy and we always ran too light a version, so they had to be carefully crack-checked every time.'

The gearshift was tortuous and featured several universal joints that were subject to severe wear, particularly on a track such as Monaco with a corner slow enough to require first gear, which had to be engaged against spring pressure. Thus the joints were regularly changed.

Exhaust systems had to be checked over for cracks and ream-welded. Again, these were prone to cracking due to vibration and the team did not have many exhaust systems on hand.

The engine would be one of the last things to reinstall due to the time that it would have

taken to overhaul. The cars may have been built on jigs but they were nowhere near as uniformly accurate as they are today. Sparshott: 'Every time you put an engine back in you might have a bit of twist – every time it was different.'

In theory, the car was now ready to roll for the next grand prix.

'This was where working for Lotus was different from working for everyone else,' says Sparshott. 'Inevitably it was "Right lads, we're going to try this or that now." You might have the car ready and be well on top of things, but then there would be changes to make. This was a constant thing, but you had to start as if you were going to run the cars as they had been for the previous grand prix – otherwise you would never have finished. Sometimes we would still be messing about when we should have been on the road to the docks.

'You would have your spec for the car. Lotus carried boxes and boxes of springs, with all the colour codes under the sun, all rates and frequencies. Colin or Maurice would decide on what was a good set of springs and the geometry settings. The major job with setting up the car was getting rid of the bump steer. If you had to take the suspension to bits, you had to prepare as best you could by measuring everything, such as the lengths between the joints of a radius rod or a wishbone, ready for when you put it back together – you then tested for bump steer.

'The final thing to do was the corner weights: we had a system of four, heavy-duty scales on a level area. Paddocks being what they were then, the level area at Hethel might be the last such area the mechanics saw until they returned to the works after the race. The corner weights were critical but we used to get them pretty good.

'Between races we used to put in a nominal amount of fuel – about five gallons – to keep the tanks wet.

'If you managed to get a clean break and go off to a race when you were supposed to, everything was pretty orderly. Where it went wrong was if you had one of those last-minute things and you would leave late at night or without enough time to get the booked boat. Then you only had time to get out of your overalls, wash your hands, grab the case you'd brought with you to work that morning, load up and go.'

At the track, of course, there were still changes that could be made: regular things like aerodynamic adjustments, shock absorbers, springs, ride height, camber settings and anti-roll bars. There were about a dozen anti-roll bars of different thicknesses available to the team, and rear bars could be adjusted. When the 49 was running with the Hewland gearbox, ratios could be changed too, whereas with the earlier ZF the whole 'box had to be changed if the ratios were wrong; in those days, therefore, the team carried about ten gearboxes.

Starting-up process

The Cosworth DFV is very sensitive to temperature. On a cold morning at a track, the mechanics would empty the water system and refill with warm water, and in unusually cold weather they would also put warm oil – with reduced viscosity – in the engine. For the first minute after starting the DFV is vulnerable to a problem that can occur if the oil is thick: in the drive system to the oil pumps there is a little clutch that is designed to slip so that undue loadings do not cause breakages within the system; when this clutch does slip, the scavenge pump ceases operation and oil cascades out of the top of the engine.

The fuel cam is checked to ensure that it is fuel-rich. There are five positions on the mechanical injection system, adjusted by a small, spring-loaded plunger down on the metering unit in the vee. Once the engine is warm, the position is changed to the central one, for medium-rich. Just before the car goes out in anger, this is altered again, to one of the two lean positions.

Team Lotus had different fuel cams for different circuits, related to atmospheric pressure. At sea level – as at Monaco – more fuel would be used and a richer cam would be required, but at relatively high-altitude circuits – such as Kyalami and Mexico City – the engine would run with a leaner cam. Changing the fuel cam was a difficult job at a circuit so it was preferable to install the right one at the factory.

The starting procedure is performed by two mechanics. The trumpet bungs are removed and a slave battery connected up. The plugs are removed and then the starter motor spun over until the oil pressure needle starts to move. The plugs are replaced and a couple of tiny squirts of fuel directed down the trumpets. Then the engine is spun again and the start button pressed by the second mechanic, who has his right hand on the throttle to help the engine fire up. If too much petrol is squirted down the trumpets, the plugs get wet and the process has to be started again.

When the engine is first started, it is essential to keep the revs low, at about 2,000rpm, until some temperature starts to show. The engine is run at about 4,000rpm once water temperature shows about 80°C and oil about 60–70°, and then run for three or four minutes until hot. This routine is carried out about an hour before the first run of the day to make sure that there are no problems. When the engine is started again, ready for action, it will do so easily, probably without the need for priming with fuel down the trumpets.

If an engine was not warmed properly there were a couple of problems that could arise on an early-specification DFV. In these engines there was a thin quill shaft that ran between the metering unit and the drive train, and this could twist – making the fuel injection timing wrong. The front belts could even break, which meant that the engine would have to come out.

BELOW **The Cosworth DFV is sensitive to temperature when starting.** *(Author)*

'If you get the chance, buy it.'

Clive Chapman
Director, Classic Team Lotus

Chapter Five

Restoration and historic racing

In June 2014 Bonhams auctioned an ex-Graham Hill Lotus 49. Thus, despite the fact that only seven genuine examples remain, it is occasionally possible to buy one. One is still owned by the Chapman family and two by museums, while four are in private hands – at least one of these is still raced.

OPPOSITE Chris MacAllister's R2/R11 has been restored to race. Here, Classic Team Lotus's team manager Chris Dinnage pedals the car around Snetterton. *(Author)*

With so few Lotus 49s produced, the chances of being able to acquire one are slim. However, an ex-Graham Hill example was auctioned in June 2014, by Bonhams at the Goodwood Festival of Speed, and achieved a price of £673,500 – a little below expectations.

The Lotus 49s that still exist are a varied group, ranging in their levels of originality and age, from early to late. There is even an example that can trace its origins back to one of the original ZF-gearbox cars, having later become a Hewland-gearbox Type 49B before being returned to its 1967 specification during restoration in recent years.

There are certain production racing cars, such as the Lola T70 or Lotus 23, where, because of the demands on historic racing, it almost seems as if there are more cars now than existed in period. While this is not the case with the Lotus 49, the potential buyer does have to be wary that a car under consideration is the real thing.

Seven genuine Lotus 49s still exist. One of these never raced, although it may contain the monocoque floor of a car that did. In addition there is a recreation that was sanctioned by Rob Walker and a copy that is not recognised as a Type 49 by Classic Team Lotus, the keeper of the Team Lotus flame.

Buying and maintaining a Lotus 49

Colin Chapman's son Clive, who runs Classic Team Lotus, reckons that his operation receives more enquiries about the Lotus 49 than any other car: 'A lot of people want one. If you get a chance, buy it!'

Chapman has noticed that the newer owners of historic racers now tend to be keen to put their cars back to how they were in period, in every detail. The ultimate example of this is Chris MacAllister, who commissioned Classic Team Lotus to rebuild his 49B, as raced in 1969, back into one of the first two 1967-spec cars.

The surviving cars range from those that are museum exhibits – at the National Motor Museum and the Donington Collection – to MacAllister's, which continues to be raced. All can be run, although some of them are only used for exhibition work and are unsuitable for racing.

As with any racing car, the value of a Lotus 49 will very much depend upon the history of the chassis, in particular who drove it and which races it won. A potential owner should, of course, check on the provenance and the trail of owners. The history of each Lotus 49 is now securely recorded after considerable study and scholarship.

Leading racing car dealer Adrian Hamilton has observed that a World Championship-winning car can be worth as much as 50 per cent more that a less successful example. With the Lotus 49, this assessment points to R5 and R6, the cars used by Graham Hill to win the world title in 1968, as being the most desirable, but the significance of Jim Clark and the early success of the DFV probably skews this observation in the case of the Lotus 49.

With the exception of Donington's R12, all Lotus 49s were raced at some stage by Jim Clark, Graham Hill or Jochen Rindt. Chassis R7 is the only one that was never a factory car, but Hill raced it after he joined Rob Walker's team and it also has great historical significance as the last privately entered car to win a World Championship grand prix. R11 only once raced as a factory car, but there is now no doubt that it was built up from R2 and it has now been returned to that original specification.

Of the survivors, the least used by any of the 'greats' is R8, which spent most of its working life firstly as a Tasman car and then in the hands of South African drivers. It only made two grand prix appearances as a factory entry, with Hill driving it on one of those occasions, at Silverstone in 1969. However, as this is the

only Lotus 49 to have gone on sale in recent years, it is the only one for which a precise value is known – £673,500 when auctioned in June 2014.

Potential purchasers of a Lotus 49 have to take into consideration the state in which they wish the car to be maintained. Should historic racing be on the agenda, safety requirements could mean considerable work and, potentially, certain departures from original specification, in which case a Historic Technical Passport (HTP) will be required.

As with any valuable car, it is important to have a potential purchase inspected by an expert. Because of the special nature of the Type 49, any problems – such as damage to the chassis or the Cosworth DFV engine being in a sorry state – need not deter the buyer, but such matters would naturally be reflected in the price paid.

A major decision will concern the state in which the new purchase is to be maintained and the amount of restoration work to be carried out. If it is to be a demonstration runner or a museum piece, then the modern trend will be to ensure that it contains as many original parts as possible, or at least parts made to original specification. This may not be possible if it is intended to race the car, but the historical significance of each Lotus 49 means that the likelihood of a car being raced is much reduced nowadays. Classic Team Lotus, for example, used to race its example, but the

company's policy now is to confine this World Championship winner's use to demonstration and exhibition work. Chris MacAllister, on the other hand, believes that racing cars were made for racing and thus his example, despite a history that can be traced back to Jim Clark's historic win at Zandvoort in 1967, is still active.

The historic racing scene is one of the most flourishing in motor sport and there are some notable opportunities for a Lotus 49 to appear in both Europe and North America. Foremost among these is the biennial Grand Prix de Monaco Historique, which started in 1997 and has, in fact, been won by a Lotus 49. The 2014 running of the event included a race for Formula 1 cars from 1966 to 1972 in which MacAllister took part in his Type 49.

ABOVE Early and late examples of the Lotus 49 – R3 and R10 – on track for the Jim Clark tribute at the Goodwood Revival in 2013. *(Author)*

BELOW R10 and R3 basking in the Goodwood sunshine. *(Author)*

Lotus 49 R8 went on sale at the Bonhams auction at the Goodwood Festival of Speed in June 2014. From late 1975 this car was part of the collection owned by John Dawson-Damer, who was killed at Goodwood in 2000 while driving his Lotus 63. Following this tragedy, Dawson-Damer's family sold most of his eight-car collection of Lotuses but chose to retain the Type 49.

James Knight, group director of Bonhams' motoring department, points out that his company had been close to the Dawson-Damer family for some years. Although British, Dawson-Damer made his home in Australia and it was felt appropriate to sell the majority of his collection in that country, something that Bonhams was able to do in 2008 through its Australian subsidiary. In 2013 the family felt the time was right for the 49 also to be passed on to a new owner.

'We did not have to look too hard to realise that our auction at the Goodwood Festival of Speed would be a wholly appropriate occasion at which to sell the car,' said Knight, who was, at the same time, sensitive to the fact that it had been at Goodwood that Dawson-Damer had had his fatal accident. The family agreed that this would be the ideal chance to realise the best possible price and Bonhams accordingly

prepared a glossy prospectus that included a history of R8.

R8 was used in both the Tasman series and the South African Drivers' Championship, but its finest hour during its limited grand prix career came when Richard Attwood took it to fourth place at Monaco in 1969. That year it raced in one other grand prix, at Silverstone, where Graham Hill finished seventh.

Still operational, the car was shipped to the UK in early 2014 and taken to Classic Team Lotus in Hethel to be prepared to what Knight describes as 'appropriate condition'. That meant, it was decided, that the car should now look as it did when Hill drove it at Silverstone – 'but we did not want to affect the car's patina or integrity'.

The car's lack of a rear wing was rectified and the mirrors repositioned. Work was also carried out on the nose so that the appropriate winglets could be fitted. Knight: 'We have tried to present the car in the best possible guise.'

R8 was then displayed in March for a press call at Bonhams in New Bond Street, London, an event attended by one of its original drivers, Richard Attwood. An estimate was put on it of between £700,000 and £1 million, but in fact the price realised fell slightly short of that range, at £673,500.

BELOW After preparation by Classic Team Lotus, Bonhams displayed R8 at its showrooms in New Bond Street, London, in March 2014 prior to auction at Goodwood three months later. *(Author)*

The Fédération Internationale de l'Automobile (FIA) sanctions a series for which the Lotus 49 is eligible: the Masters Historic Racing Formula 1 championship catering for 3-litre cars from 1966 to 1985. It has a class-based structure, with categories named after champions of the period, the oldest cars, such as the Lotus 49, being in the Stewart class. All cars entered have to be presented with a current HTP and all DFV engines used are restricted to a rev limit of 10,000rpm. Drivers must be in possession of a current racing licence with a minimum MSA International C or ASN equivalent. Entrants have the opportunity to race at a number of historic venues. For example, the calendar for 2014 included Barcelona, Brands Hatch, Brno, Silverstone, the Nürburgring, Zandvoort, Spa and Jerez.

An important factor for any owner is insurance. This will depend upon the use that is going to be made of the car and should be placed with an insurance company that understands motor sport. Two types of insurance are available: the first is for a car stored and in transit between circuits as well as garaged by the owner when not in use, and the second is for a car to be run on a track. The latter, of course, will be more expensive and will usually require the policyholder to accept a high excess, of around 15–20 per cent of the car's value.

Because of the importance of any Lotus 49, it should be covered under a specialist policy that offers an agreed insurance value should it be damaged beyond economic repair. Known as an 'agreed-value policy', this removes any doubt over the value of the car in the event of a claim. While it is obvious that, with so few Lotus 49s in existence, every attempt would be made to repair a damaged one, it should not be forgotten that one of the original cars was totally destroyed in a workshop fire – something that could happen again.

Restored and preserved examples

R2/R11: Chris MacAllister

When discussing the provenance of historic racing cars, restorer and leading racer Simon Hadfield may point to Theseus's paradox. This asks whether an object that has had all of its components replaced remains the same object. First put in ancient Greek times, it is based on the story of a ship that, over time, had all of its planks replaced. Was it still the same ship? Such is the way in which a racing car may evolve that the paradox can become complex – and such is the case with Chris MacAllister's R2/R11.

There is, however no doubt, after much

LEFT Colin Chapman's daughter Jane Payton and her husband, Will, push Chris MacAllister's R2/R11 onto the grid at the Classic Team Lotus Festival. (Author)

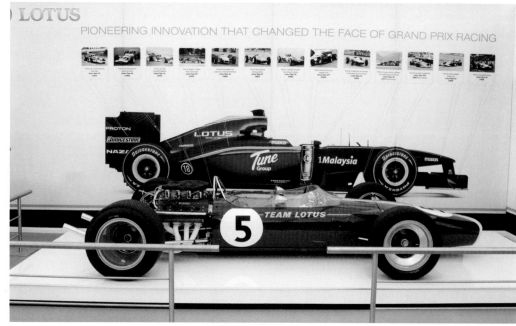

investigation, that the Lotus 49 maintained in Indianapolis by Chris MacAllister has its origins in Jim Clark's 1967 Dutch Grand Prix-winning R2. What MacAllister bought, though, was Pete Lovely's R11. Lovely acquired his Lotus 49, which was given chassis number R11, in late 1968, and Allan McCall, who had been the mechanic on R2 in 1967 (see Chapter Four), was present at Brands Hatch when Leo Wybrott delivered the car to the American.

McCall assisted in unloading it and felt that there was something familiar about it. A decade later he had the opportunity to study the car at Watkins Glen and became certain that it was based on R2.

'The pedal access hatch on R2 was smaller than on R1 or R3,' observes McCall, 'and the fuel filler is outside the plate covering the hatch. Only R2 was modified in this way, and I also don't believe that any of the subsequent cars had this fuelling and access plate arrangement. The screen on the Lovely car is correct for this fuel-intake arrangement and has early roll-over bar cut-outs, and the monocoque also has bracket holes for the early type of roll-over bar. This monocoque also has nut plates in it that I put in it to retain the fabricated shoulder rest that Jimmy used; old Frank made this in the metal fabrication department and Jimmy really rated it.

'Before the US Grand Prix the front lower wishbone mounting brackets inside the chassis were taken out and strengthened on R2. This required the front third of the monocoque to be reskinned. The Lovely car also has holes in the lower rear of the monocoque for the early radius rod arm brackets, which were on the side skin.'

Lovely could not understand why his car showed green paint on the underside when it was stripped for a repaint. This underlined the fact that R11 was based on one of the early cars, as there was never a green works 49 after R2 was painted with Gold Leaf colours at Wigram in New Zealand in January 1968.

The present owner acquired the car, which has since been 'track-tested' by Caterham Formula 1 reserve driver Alexander Rossi for *Road & Track* magazine, in 2009 as a perfect example of a late 1960s Lotus 49B. However, as R11, it had been raced by Pete Lovely on all but one occasion and was inevitably worth less than other Lotus 49s of greater significance

– but as R2, of course, it had considerable significance. In 2010, therefore, MacAllister commissioned Classic Team Lotus to rebuild the car to resemble the specification of R2, complete with change of gearbox from Hewland to ZF. National Motor Museum manager Doug Hill has claimed that R2 is not as original a 1967 car as Beaulieu's R3, although Clive Chapman pointed out that its monocoque, at least, is 'remarkably' so. In its present form the car also revives memories of Jim Clark in a way that no red, white and gold car could ever do. Its specification is also closer to the 'works' than any other Type 49 today.

The rebuild was placed in the hands of Kevin Smith at Classic Team Lotus and the task was solely his apart from the last few days of work, when everyone had to help to get the car ready for its first race appearance, at Monaco. 'Otherwise it was my baby,' Smith recalls, 'and I did about 95 per cent of it. We received the car during the Christmas of 2008, I started it in January and finished in May. Nothing much had been done to it since Pete Lovely had last raced it in 49B form.'

The brief was to present the car in 1967 Watkins Glen specification. This enabled use to be made of the period windscreen, the ignition box on the vee of the engine, and the ex-works gearbox with its strengthened sides. The owner is also a US citizen.

'It involved a lot of work and the original drawings were a big help,' continues Smith. 'A complete strip-down to the bare shell was carried out. The shell was then soda-blasted. The wishbone pick-ups were different so those were altered and rear lower wishbone mountings added. The electric fuel pump was on the left-hand side inside the monocoque on the 1967 car so that was fabricated in. Roll hoops, front and rear suspension, radiator, water system and oil system were all changed. The dash was also changed, as that was slightly different. The gearbox was replaced with a ZF version but the engine was retained. New wheels were made. Finally it was painted in the green and yellow livery and sign-written.'

A major step came when, said Clive Chapman, 'Bob Dance went down to the hangar and found two ZF gearboxes that we didn't know we had.'

After a shakedown on the Hethel test track, the car went straight into a truck for the journey to Monaco. Practice went well but in the race the ZF 'box got stuck into just two gears – a common fault in the day.

R3: National Motor Museum, Beaulieu

Doug Hill, manager at the National Motor Museum, Beaulieu, describes R3 as 'the only genuine original 49', the others from 1967 having been converted or destroyed. Because of its post-works existence in South Africa, R3 was never rebuilt to 49B specification and has always been fitted with a ZF gearbox.

A dealer called Michael Lavers brought the car back from South Africa in an original but sorry state and painted powder blue. Extensive restoration was carried out before it passed to a Japanese collector, who sold it to Beaulieu in 1985.

Hill states that R3 has had a 'hard life' but now it spends most of its time in the museum's main exhibition hall, apart from occasional outings. The National Motor Museum is a charitable trust and, says Hill, 'we can only run when we have the budget. We have to be

very careful where we spend money. We don't bother with any set-up: we don't know anything about it and it is never going to be raced.'

Drivers have included Tiff Needell, Dick Scammell, Rob Hall and Doug Hill himself. Unfortunately, the car has been crashed twice, by the same driver. The first time was on the Beaulieu estate when a misfire brought about a freak incident, which pitched the car into a tree and twisted the monocoque. Hall & Fowler, as the company was called at the time, carried out an excellent repair, retaining almost all of the monocoque. The car also features an early DFV. Hill: 'Hall & Fowler found as much early stuff as they could when they rebuilt it for us.'

A second crash occurred at the press day for the 2009 Silverstone Classic, this being blamed on the vagaries of the ZF gearbox. 'It's the only real problem we have with the car,' says Hill. 'It selects any gear apart from the one you want, although it is supposed to be semi-sequential. It has a funny little gate selector but some of the problem can be operator error. I still don't understand why it does what it does. It's all to do with the linkage.'

Apart from the ZF 'box, Ian 'Stan' Stanfield, the museum's senior workshop engineer, says,

RIGHT R3 showing features of its near-original specification. *(Author)*

'The car is normally as good as gold. There is not a lot to do on it because it is so simple. Lotus did not make it very complicated.'

Stanfield recalls an occasion when broadcaster and racing driver Tiff Needell was to demonstrate R3 at Snetterton for the *Top Gear* television programme. 'We expected to run for about five laps, so a limited amount of fuel was filled. On arrival, we discovered that the car was needed for around 30 laps. Mike Costin and Keith Duckworth were there. I said to them that we didn't have enough fuel. Mike said go down the road and buy some four-star, which I did. We tend to run it on AvGas.'

R3 is not the first Lotus 49 to have been exhibited at the National Motor Museum. R6 was on loan to Beaulieu between 1972 and 1985, a period during which the car's ownership changed from Team Lotus to Robs

BELOW Tiff Needell is entrusted to drive Beaulieu's Lotus 49. *(Author)*

Lamplough. In 1985 it went to Paris for an exhibition and was acquired there by collector Jacques Setton. It never returned.

The National Motor Museum tells the story of motor cars and the feeling there was that the Lotus 49 had a significant place in motoring history. 'It's such an iconic car,' says Hill. 'When we were told that R3 was coming up for sale, having been in Japan, we had to be interested. It was going up for auction, which normally does not work for us; as a museum we need lead time to get the funding required. However, there are various revenue streams that can be tapped into and we were able to acquire the car. I remember what a "wow" it was for it to be here.'

R7: Geoff Farmer

R7 has a somewhat unusual home, sitting as it does behind the sofa in a living room at Geoff Farmer's Derbyshire house. Perhaps that is an unfair description, as Farmer has paid suitable homage to the 1968 British Grand Prix winner with an additional room to his house that can double up as a small cinema. Through his ownership of R7, Farmer also came to know Rob Walker.

Farmer's affair with R7 started in early 1999.

The Goodwood Revival organisers were talking of running a race for pre-1968 grand prix cars, such a contest having also taken place in Adelaide with another promised for 2000. An experienced club racer, Farmer wanted to be involved. The Rob Walker Lotus 49 was coming up for auction and Farmer, who had already raced Cedric Selzer's ex-Jim Clark Lotus-Climax 25, deliberated over whether he could justify bidding for it.

Farmer was suffering from a severe migraine when he arrived at the H&H auction, which took place at the Buxton Pavilion that July. He recalled, 'The pavilion was hot, sticky, thronged with some hundreds of people, and in front of the stage on an elevated platform there was a totally unloved, uncared for, horribly neglected and engineless Lotus 49. In less than a minute, I knew there and then I was certifiably insane. But I equally knew a Lotus 49 could win at Adelaide and Goodwood.'

Auctions were nothing new to Farmer, who regularly attends them for the engineering company he runs. This, though, was something different; he felt physically ill at the thought of what he might be about to do. Over the first couple of minutes the bidding for the appropriately numbered lot 49 was brisk. It then stalled and, at the last moment, Farmer moved in with his one and only bid, upping the ante by £25,000. The next he knew, he had paid £350,000 for the car and was asking historic racer and restorer Simon Hadfield if he could arrange its collection. The Goodwood Revival was seven and a half weeks away.

Hadfield took on the 'ridiculously impossible' challenge of restoring the car in time and an original DFV was acquired for engine tuner Dick Langford to prepare for the race. Clive Chapman loaned a pair of front wheels, R7 having been bought with 49C-specification front wheels.

Hadfield found signs of the car's hard life: a lower exhaust pipe contained a dent that probably dated back to Graham Hill's practice crash at Monaco in 1970; a radius rod had broken on that occasion and the impression in the exhaust would have been caused when it was hit by the wheel rim. There was also evidence of work that had been done on the rear anti-roll bar, which Hadfield noticed a couple of days after Farmer bought the car.

LEFT Geoff Farmer's R7 is certainly a most cherished car. *(Author)*

Someone had filed various 'flats' along the bar to make it softer. Quite when this would have been done remains a mystery. As Tony Cleverly has since pointed out, it was certainly not the kind of adjustment that the Rob Walker team would have made.

Seven weeks after the auction, Farmer again had a raging headache but the car was ready to be shaken down at a damp, grey Mallory Park. 'In less than a couple of yards, I couldn't believe a car could be so bad. There was absolutely no front grip, the brakes grabbed, the pedal

BELOW R7 follows R3 in a Lotus demonstration at the Goodwood Revival meeting in 2000. *(Author)*

RIGHT Dent on the exhaust of R7, probably caused when a rear wheel became detached during Graham Hill's 1970 Monaco Grand Prix practice crash. *(Author)*

BELOW R7's rear anti-roll bar has been flattened in a number of places, presumably in an attempt to soften it. *(Author)*

went long, the understeer was bad, and the oil pressure light came on after less than a lap.' The work list at the end of the session was huge and there was less than a day before the car needed to make its way to Sussex.

Hadfield and his team worked hard but the nightmare continued. The Friday practice at Goodwood saw Farmer in last place. Huge understeer was still very apparent and the engine appeared 'wrecked'. Langford arrived from Wellingborough and looked for damage; none was evident so there had to be an installation problem.

'Simon Hadfield had reasoned that oil was getting dumped into the integral oil catch tank,' recalls Farmer, 'effectively emptying the main oil tank. The gearbox-mounted tank was removed, drained, systematically blanked and pressure-tested. Hissing of air from within revealed that Simon had located the problem area. Out came hacksaws and a four-inch square section [now another permanent part of this car's history] was cut and flapped upwards to reveal a long, gaping crack in the internal ¾in aluminium oil return pipe. The time was now 5.30pm. We located probably the only expert TIG welder in Chichester and he worked stoically to repair the pipe and patch the tank. Simon and his team reassembled everything, and by 10pm reported success. The engine seemed OK and the oil pressure light was staying out.'

Hadfield was preoccupied the next morning with his own driving, in a Lotus 48, and Jon Spooner took over responsibility for the car. The work done by the indefatigable team was now paying off as R7 completed its first flying lap in 29 years. The handling was still not right and Spooner put on more rear bar. Still it was not quite right, so he softened the front dampers, stiffened the rears and put on all the rear bar possible. Having completed seven or eight laps, Farmer noticed that Keith Duckworth and Dick Scammell, who had been talking on his pit counter, were smiling. He was on pole.

The race itself featured two former Lotus 49 drivers in Jackie Oliver and Richard Attwood, with Oliver in a 49, albeit David McLaughlin's recreation. The race was marred by Jack Brabham's accident, which caused a stoppage, but after the restart Farmer won a famous victory, setting a new outright lap record for

LEFT This 4in square repair in R7's oil tank has become a permanent part of its history. *(Author)*

Goodwood in the process, the previous holders having been Jim Clark and Jackie Stewart.

Farmer also raced the car the following year at Adelaide Parklands. Three 49s were entered for the three 'Formula Adelaide' races that weekend – part of the Clipsal 500 meeting – and Farmer won the first, with Pete Lovely second in R11, the car he had raced in period, and John Dawson-Damer seventh in R8. The second race saw Farmer again beat Lovely, with Dawson-Damer sixth this time. In the final race the top two positions were reversed and Dawson-Damer came fourth.

R10: Classic Team Lotus

A Lotus 49 remains in the Chapman family's hands as part of the outstanding collection held by Classic Team Lotus. The car in question is R10, the renumbered R5, and it is still in original condition. Eddie Dennis, who worked on the 49s in period, rebuilt it and many years after it had won at Monaco, in 1968 as R5 and in 1969 as R10, the car returned to the street circuit again, this time for the Historic Grand Prix in 1997. It competed on a couple of other occasions as an historic racer, using a Langford-serviced DFV, but it was then decided that its competition days were over.

R10 is still often seen in public, and in 2012 it defied gravity as part of the Lotus sculpture that dominated that year's Goodwood Festival

of Speed. Latter-day display drivers have included Mario Andretti, Jackie Oliver and Emerson Fittipaldi, all of whom drove this car in period, the first two when it was R5, the latter three times when it was known as R10. Damon and Josh Hill have also both demonstrated it; Chapman, incidentally, observed that Oliver is 'very careful with the car'. It has even appeared in a Robbie Williams video, *Supreme*, and on the BBC's *Top of the Pops*.

Joaquin Folch-Rusiñol, the leading historic racer and Spanish businessman, was the driver when R10 returned to Monaco in 1997. 'I was one of the first people to drive Clive's 49 and for me it was a big moment. I first went to Snetterton to test the car and then we went to Monaco, where we were happy to win.

'The 49 was special for me. During the Spanish Grand Prix in 1969, my father was at the marshals' post just where Jochen Rindt's accident happened, with his close friend Bernard Cahier. I have pictures of my father taking Rindt out of the car.

'I started on pole for the Monaco race and managed to get to Ste Devote first, with Geoff Farmer on my tail, as well as a Ferrari test driver in a V12 Ferrari, and for a couple of laps we fight very strong. I was defending my position but then gradually I just went away.

'It was brutal to drive. Cars of that period are really difficult to drive because the V8 Cosworth

RIGHT R10 was part of the Jim Clark tribute at the 2013 Goodwood Revival meeting. Chris MacAllister did not bring his own R2/11, but guested at the wheel of the CTL car. *(Author)*

has lots of power but there is no aerodynamic help at all and no slicks. To drift those cars is something very special. I also drove it at one of the Lotus Festivals at Brands Hatch and, the following year, at the Goodwood Revival, where I spun in the early stages.'

R12: Donington Collection

Chassis R12 may not have the illustrious history of the other Lotus 49s but it is on permanent display for the general public to see. It was originally delivered, in 49B specification, to the Ford Motor Company in late 1968, soon making a first appearance at the Racing Car Show in Olympia. Ford used it as a promotional vehicle before donating it to the Donington Collection in Derbyshire, where it has resided ever since. Lotus historian Michael Oliver believes the monocoque floor may have been used for a genuine race car at some time, possibly as part of R6 that Jackie Oliver crashed in France.

When acquired, the car was a somewhat untypical choice for Tom Wheatcroft, founder of the Donington Collection, for he had mainly been collecting cars of the 1940s and 1950s; by contrast the Lotus 49 was almost a contemporary car when the museum opened in 1973. It is exhibited with the later low wing,

RIGHT R10 featured on the sculpture outside Goodwood House during the 2012 Festival of Speed. *(Author)*

but a high-mounted aerofoil is also on display behind the car. The car is not a runner, although it is thought that there were once plans, when Wheatcroft was alive, to get it working.

'Outings are rare,' says Donington's managing director, Christopher Tate, 'the idea being to keep it in a time capsule.' It did venture out in 2013, though, when it was sent to the Sky Sports television studio for a programme. With tongue slightly in cheek, Tate adds, 'The car is what it is but its provenance since it arrived in the collection is immaculate.'

For Tate the Lotus 49 has particular meaning as his father, Johnny, was a close friend of Rob Walker. That meant that the Tate family were guests of the famous entrant at the 1968 British Grand Prix, where, as recorded elsewhere, Jo Siffert won in Walker's Lotus 49. 'We were watching and suddenly there was "Seppe" with a real chance of winning.'

'Not a bad old tool.'
Graham Hill
Team Lotus driver

Chapter Six

Individual chassis histories

Ten Lotus 49 monocoques were built, although one of these was never raced. Of the nine that competed, only one was considered beyond repair following a crash, although another was destroyed in a workshop fire. There are, therefore, seven Type 49s with race history in existence. A Team Lotus policy of renumbering monocoques, particularly after a major rebuild, has meant that three of the ten have dual identities, and there were two R6s.

OPPOSITE Graham Hill could usually be relied upon to star in the Monaco Grand Prix – here he is with R5 on his way to winning the 1968 race. *(Ford)*

A total of ten Lotus 49 monocoques were created and even one of these was almost certainly built using the remains of another. However, chassis numbers wrongly suggest that 12 existed. This discrepancy was the result of Lotus's policy at the time of salvaging and restoring cars and then renumbering them – which can cause confusion. For example, the 1967 Dutch Grand Prix winner, R2, was rebuilt and sold to privateer Pete Lovely as R11. When it was acquired by Chris MacAllister it was restored to its original specification and now appears as it did when it was R2.

In addition to the seven raced Lotus 49s that still remain, there exists a recreation of Rob Walker's 49/R4. This was completed in the late 1990s by Hall & Fowler for a consortium led by David McLaughlin. The project was sanctioned by Walker and his 49B/R7 used as a template. Fitted with a ZF gearbox, it was originally in Walker blue but was later repainted in Gold Leaf Team Lotus colours and, in 2008, sold to an anonymous Japanese collector. A replica was also competed by Hall & Hall in 2008 for Peter and John Morley, and then sold to Portuguese lawyer Rodrigo Gallego. However, unlike the 49/R4 recreation, which had a 'virtual' link back to a real car, this replica is not recognised by Classic Team Lotus and the owner was formally requested to remove the Lotus name, badge and chassis plate.

BELOW The chief mechanics were expected to be able to drive the cars. This is Dick Scammell in R1 near the beginning of the story. (Ford)

49/R1, 49T/R1 (later 49T/R9, 49B/R9)

R1 was the prototype 49 that was first raced by Graham Hill in the 1967 Dutch Grand Prix. The Englishman raced the car on 11 occasions, winning on his last appearance with the car, the 1968 Spanish Grand Prix. Jim Clark used it just twice, winning on both occasions, the 1967 Mexican and Spanish Grands Prix, the latter a non-championship race. It was also Hill's mount for the 1968 Tasman series, albeit only for the Australian races. For this it assumed 49T form, which meant that it used the 2½-litre version of the DFV, the DFW.

This car's history also illustrates the way in which Team Lotus sometimes employed a third driver, usually a local, paying one. Eppie Wietzes, Giancarlo Baghetti and Moises Solana all drove R1. Jackie Oliver also made his grand prix début in it, crashing on the first lap of the 1968 Monaco Grand Prix. It was only the second time the car had been in a major accident, the first being Hill's practice shunt at Silverstone the year before that had resulted in frantic work to build up a replacement car for the British Grand Prix the next day.

Following Oliver's crash, R1 was rebuilt for 1969, first as a 49T for the Tasman races and then as a 49B. As such, it was renumbered 49B/R9.

49/R2, 49T/R2, 49B/R2 (later 49B/R11)

This is arguably the most famous of all Lotus 49s – the one with which Jim Clark won the 1967 Dutch Grand Prix. The Scot also won with it at Silverstone and Watkins Glen before it was converted to 49T specification and taken to the Tasman series, where he won four races and the title.

After Rob Walker's R4 had been destroyed in a workshop fire early in 1968, R2 was lent to Walker for Jo Siffert to drive. The Swiss had a torrid time with the car, which was returned to the factory prior to the British Grand Prix when Walker's new car, R7, was ready. R2 was then converted to 49B specification using some of the parts from R6, which Oliver had crashed at Rouen. Oliver now used R2 himself for the latter

part of the 1968 season. The only other driver to race R2 was the Mexican, Moises Solana.

At the end of the 1968 season, R2 was updated with a more substantial roll-over hoop and fire extinguisher system. On being acquired by American Pete Lovely, it was renumbered R11.

49/R3

It might be said that R3's first appearance in the world was a dramatic one. It was this car that was hurriedly finished, along with its strange, temporary nose, for the 1967 British Grand Prix. It differed substantially from its predecessors in that it was made of heavier-gauge aluminium sheet and featured an additional 'baffle' bulkhead at the front of the monocoque, together with a combined access hatch and fuel filler, and longer fairings behind the rocker arms. All subsequent 49s were built this way while R1 and R2 were converted mid-season.

Despite its fraught beginnings, R3 led its first race, driven by Hill. The Londoner drove it on eight occasions that season, with three second places its best finishes; he also badly damaged it in practice at the Nürburgring.

R3's winning ways began the following year after it had been sold to Rhodesian John Love, who replaced the ZF gearbox with a Hewland FG400 at the end of the season. Competing with it in the South African Drivers'

ABOVE R2 was Jim Clark's mount for 1967. *(Ford)*

Championship, Love finished first on 13 occasions, taking the title in 1968 and '69. The car was then sold to Peter Parnell, who raced it during the latter part of 1970. However, Parnell defaulted on payments and Love took the car back. It then languished for around a decade before being brought back to the UK by dealer Michael Lavers and extensively restored. Japanese collector Yoshiyuki Hayashi then owned it for a period, during which it appeared

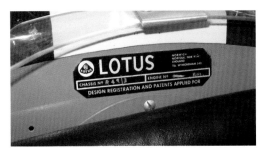

LEFT Chassis plate indicating the identity of the National Motor Museum's Lotus 49. *(Andy Brown)*

BELOW This is R3, looking strange with unfamiliar nose following its rapid rebuild for the 1967 British Grand Prix. *(LAT Phtographic)*

in a couple of historic events at Suzuka and Fuji, before it was sold in 1985 to the National Motor Museum at Beaulieu.

The car is now regularly seen in the UK back in green and yellow and looking the epitome of an early Type 49. Two accidents occurred during demonstrations in 1998 and 2009, reducing its on-track activity. After the first accident, Hall & Fowler carried out a careful restoration.

49/R4

R4 took part in just one race, which it won. It was Clark's mount for his final grand prix victory, the 1968 South African Grand Prix. Then it was sold to the Rob Walker/Jack Durlacher team and entered for the Race of Champions at Brands Hatch, where it was badly damaged when Siffert crashed it in unofficial practice. It was returned to Walker's garage where, the next day, it was destroyed in an accidental fire that engulfed the premises.

49/R5, 49B/R5 (later 49B/R10, 49C/R10)

R5 was built at the end of the 1967 season and its first public appearance, without an engine, was at the press announcement of John

ABOVE One race, one win – the 1968 South African Grand Prix was R4's only outing. *(sutton-images.com)*

RIGHT The story of R5 itemised in Bob Dance's notebook.

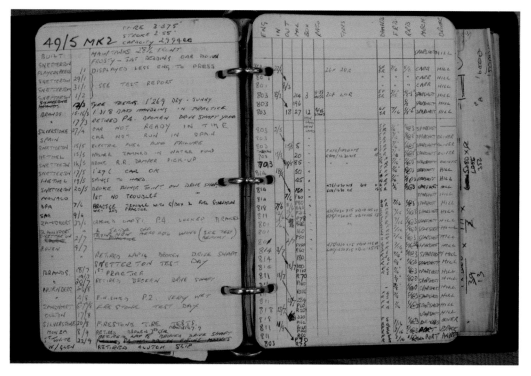

Player Gold Leaf sponsorship. It was raced just once – by Hill at the 1968 Race of Champions – in its early guise, with a ZF gearbox, before being dismantled and rebuilt into the first Type 49B, with a Hewland gearbox.

Hill raced R5 in seven grands prix in 1968 and won one of them, in Monte Carlo. For the last four races of the season it was used by Jackie Oliver (twice), Bill Brack and Mario Andretti. It was this car that Andretti put on pole at Watkins Glen, a feat Hill also achieved with it at the Monaco and British Grands Prix, and at Oulton Park for the non-championship Gold Cup.

Like R2, R5 was modified at the end of the 1968 season to meet new regulations concerning the roll-over hoop and fire extinguisher, and it was renumbered R10. As such, Hill won with it again at Monaco, in 1969.

49B/R6 (both monocoques), 49C/R6

R6 was the first Type 49B to be built from scratch, rather than modified from an earlier car. In theory it did not last long, as it was written off when Oliver crashed at Rouen in 1968. It is believed that the monocoque may have been used much later to form the basis of R12, which was never raced. Some of the

salvageable parts were also used for R7. Further parts, and the chassis plate, became part of a 'new' R6 – there was nothing new in reusing a chassis plate to overcome customs regulations.

The 'new' R6 was Hill's car for eight races, Graham winning with it in Mexico. It became Jochen Rindt's regular mount for 1969 and the early part of 1970, when it was brought up to Type 49C specification. It cemented its place in history by being the car with which he won the 1969 US and 1970 Monaco Grands Prix.

Following one-off appearances with Alex Soler-Roig and Wilson Fittipaldi, R6 became the last 49 to be raced by the factory when Tony Trimmer used it at Oulton Park in 1971. After the end of its factory career, the car was eventually sold to Robs Lamplough in a controversial transaction. After spells in the ownership of Frenchman Jacques Setton and American Bruce McCaw, it was acquired, in 2003, by Austrian Joe Willenpart, who had the car rebuilt in the UK by Hall & Hall.

49B/R7, 49C/R7

R7 was the second of Rob Walker's own 49s, replacing R4, which had been destroyed in the workshop fire, and the new car arrived with the team after a spell in which it

BELOW **Jochen Rindt in R6 battled with Jackie Stewart for the 1969 British Grand Prix. Note the damaged wing end plate** (Ford)

ABOVE Graham Hill took over R7 when Jo Siffert left Rob Walker to join March for 1970. *(Ford)*

BELOW Despite a long and active life, R8 was only twice entered by the factory for a grand prix. The 1969 Montjuich Park disaster meant that it had to be brought into action for Richard Attwood for the Monaco Grand Prix despite, apart from the engine, still being in Tasman trim. *(Ford)*

raced R2 on loan from the factory. On delivery, R7 differed from the factory cars in that it sported smaller nose fins and a lower rear wing. On its début at the 1968 British Grand Prix, driven by Jo Siffert, it became the last independently entered car ever to win a World Championship grand prix. The Swiss driver raced the immaculately prepared, dark blue car for the rest of the season and throughout 1969, and then it was used by Graham Hill when he joined the team in 1970.

After retirement it became the property of the Walker Family Trust, going on display at the Donington Collection. It was sold at auction in 1999 and acquired by Geoff Farmer.

49/R8(T), 49B/R8, 49C/R8

R8, together with R9, was built for the 1969 Tasman series. It initially incorporated some of the features of the 49, including a ZF gearbox, as well as aspects of the 49B. This hybrid car, however, proved troublesome for Hill in the races 'down under' and was sent home unloved.

Following the crashes in the 1969 Spanish Grand Prix, it had to be pressed into Formula 1 service – which meant retrieving it from Southampton docks upon its return from Australia – and prepared for the Monaco Grand Prix for Richard Attwood to drive. A 3-litre engine was installed but very little else was done to the car for the race, in which Attwood finished fourth. After Monaco it was converted to full Type 49B specification, complete with Hewland gearbox.

R8 was then sold to Swedish driver Jo Bonnier. When Hill refused to race a four-wheel-drive Type 63 in the 1969 British Grand Prix at Silverstone, the car was borrowed back for Team Lotus to run in that one event. Bonnier competed in just one grand prix with it before crashing the car at Oulton Park and returning it to the factory, where it was repossessed.

Fitted with new fabricated uprights and 13in wheels to bring it up to Type 49C specification, R8 was subsequently bought by Dave Charlton to use in the South African Drivers' Championship, which he won in 1970 and '71, racing it no fewer than 20 times; during his second season he did six of the championship's ten races in R8 before changing to a Lotus 72. Peter de Klerk then took over the driving before an argument with Charlton caused him to leave the team, Meyer Botha then stepping in for the car's last two races, the second of which finished in a major accident.

In late 1975 Charlton sold R8 to Australia-based John Dawson-Damer, who was tragically killed at Goodwood in 2000 in his Lotus 63. The ownership of R8, which had now been rebuilt by him in Sydney, passed to his daughter Adelicia. In June 2014 it was sold at the Bonhams auction at Goodwood.

49T/R9, 49B/R9

While R8 was a completely new car, its sister for the 1969 Tasman series, R9, was a rebuild of R1, the very first chassis. Like R8, it was built as a 2½-litre 49T and was a hybrid with ZF gearbox, combined oil/water radiator, oil tank in the nose and earlier suspension.

Its career was short and sweet, always with Jochen Rindt at the wheel. After two races in New Zealand, the second ending with a monocoque-damaging accident, R9 was rebuilt as a Type 49B for the South African Grand Prix and a couple of non-championship events before being wrecked at Montjuich Park. It was considered beyond repair and thrown into a skip – the only Type 49 to be so condemned.

49B/R10, 49C/R10

The first of the 49Bs, R5, was renumbered during the winter of 1968. Quite why is not apparent as it was not modified. With a 2½-litre DFV engine but otherwise unchanged, it was shipped 'down under' as a replacement for Rindt's crashed R9. It was clearly a better car than the surviving 49T, R8, and Hill used it to win two races. It was not raced again until after the accidents in Spain, Hill taking it over for the rest of the season and winning at Monte Carlo.

Following Hill's accident at Watkins Glen at the end of 1969, R10 was rebuilt and converted to Type 49C specification. A variety of drivers raced it in 1970, including Emerson Fittipaldi (who made his grand prix début with the car), John Miles and Alex Soler-Roig. When Miles failed to qualify at

ABOVE R9 had a short life before being written off at Montjuich Park. Here Siffert in R7 passes the two wrecked Team Lotus cars. *(Ford)*

BELOW At Brands Hatch in 1970 Emerson Fittipaldi made his grand prix début in R10. *(Ford)*

Monte Carlo, it was repainted in Rob Walker blue and reunited with Hill for the third successive year in Monaco, as Hill had a guaranteed position on the grid for that race.

R10 is the one Type 49 to have remained in the possession of the Chapman family and is now operated by Classic Team Lotus. It was rebuilt by Eddie Dennis, who had worked on 49s in period, and Chris Dinnage. In 1997 it reappeared, most appropriately, for the Historic Grand Prix at Monaco, where it had won in 1968 (as R5) and 1969 (as R10), and it was victorious again, driven by Joaquin Folch-Rusiñol.

49B/R11

R11 is another of the renumbered chassis, for this was originally R2, the 1967 Dutch Grand Prix winner. Having been updated to 1969 specification, the car was sold early that season to American Pete Lovely, who had a long-established link with Lotus in that he had tried to qualify a works Lotus 16 for the 1959 Monaco Grand Prix. The number eleven was next in the Type 49 sequence and ideally suited Lovely: his wife, Nevele ('eleven' spelt backwards), was said to have been born on the eleventh minute of the eleventh hour of the eleventh day of November.

BELOW **This Type 49 was known as R11 during the period when Pete Lovely owned it.**
(Ford)

Prior to Lovely taking delivery of the car, Mario Andretti drove it in the South African Grand Prix. It was then hastily resprayed using the red from the Gold Leaf colour scheme. The car had an eclectic time with Lovely, initially taking in the two UK non-championship races before being shipped to the USA, where it was given the US colours of white and blue. That year it took in the three grands prix in the Americas as well as a number of rounds of the SCCA's Formula A championship.

Lovely tried to qualify for some grands prix in 1970 both in Europe and North America, but he only made the grid for Brands Hatch. For the following season, he grafted the back end of the 49 on to a Formula 2 Lotus 69, racing this in the Canadian and US Grands Prix but failing to be classified on both occasions.

The Lotus 49 remained in Lovely's ownership until 2006 and was eventually restored for historic racing. Bob Baker then purchased it and sold it three years later to Indianapolis-based Chris MacAllister. It was sent to Classic Team Lotus, returned to 'works' 1967 specification and reunited with a ZF gearbox, thus resembling Clark's 1967 Dutch Grand Prix car, albeit as it had been when it won the US Grand Prix that year.

49/R12

'Never raced' is how R12 might be advertised if it ever went up for sale. The car was built as a promotional vehicle for Ford, which took delivery of it in late 1968. It toured extensively before being donated to the Donington Grand Prix Collection.

Lotus historian Michael Oliver believes that R12 is based around the remains of R6, the car Jackie Oliver crashed at Rouen in 1968. Initially it was fitted with a ZF gearbox although an oil tank was mounted over the 'box, thus making it look more like a Type 49B. Eventually it was converted to full 49B specification with a Hewland 'box.

The private entries

As already noted, the Lotus 49 has a place in history as the last car to win a World Championship Grand Prix for a privately entered team. There was still nothing unusual in an independent entry in 1968. The day Jo Siffert won the British Grand Prix in the R.R.C. Walker & J.S. Durlacher car, the Charles Vogele Team, Reg Parnell and Ecurie Bonnier also had cars on the grid. The non-championship Formula 1 events that still existed in the late 1960s gave further opportunities for such teams.

Five independent teams entered Lotus 49s for World Championship rounds. Of these, the Rob Walker équipe was easily the most prominent. The others were the driver/owners Jo Bonnier, Pete Lovely, John Love and Dave Charlton.

Rob Walker

Rob Walker, of the Johnnie Walker whisky family, who described his occupation on his passport as 'gentleman', was easily the most successful private entrant in the history of the Formula 1 World Championship, winning nine races between 1958 and 1968, seven of them with Stirling Moss.

In 1964, Walker first employed Jo Siffert as one of his drivers. The Swiss remained with the team until the end of 1969, the last two years with Lotus 49s. Prior to that Siffert had driven a 1½-litre Brabham and then a 3-litre Cooper-Maserati T81 for Walker. Former Team Lotus driver Graham Hill joined Walker for 1970,

ABOVE The never-raced R12 on display at the Racing Car Show, Olympia, London. *(Ferret Fotographics)*

BELOW The remains of Rob Walker's first Lotus 49 and his Cooper-Maserati the day after the fire. *(Ferret Fotographics)*

LEFT Tony Cleverly (left) and Jean-Pierre Oberson pour fuel into the Rob Walker Lotus 49 at Watkins Glen. *(Tony Cleverly collection)*

initially driving the 49 before his Lotus 72 was ready. Between 1966 and 1969 stockbroker Jack Durlacher was a partner in Walker's team.

The always smartly attired Walker used four Lotus 49s, all painted in his usual dark blue, Scottish livery. The first, 49/R4, had the shortest life of any Type 49. It only did one race, the 1968 South African Grand Prix, which it won as a Team Lotus entry for Jim Clark. Walker then entered it for the Brands Hatch Race of Champions, where Siffert crashed in a pre-practice session. It was returned to the team's workshop, where it was destroyed in a fire.

The factory then loaned the team R2, which Siffert raced on six occasions, until a replacement car, R7, was ready. R7, which won the British Grand Prix on its début, was the only Type 49 never to be raced by Team Lotus. Siffert and Hill used it extensively from mid-1968 to mid-1970, and Siffert twice finished in a podium position with it during 1969.

Walker also used the works car R10 at the 1970 Monaco Grand Prix after Hill – a graded driver with a guaranteed position on the grid – damaged R7 in practice. When factory driver John Miles failed to qualify in R10, the car was hastily repainted blue for Hill to race the following day.

Jo Bonnier

The only other European to run a Lotus 49 was 1959 Dutch Grand Prix winner Jo Bonnier. The Swedish journeyman had experienced a reasonably successful Formula 1 career since 1956 and during that time had driven for Maserati, BRM and Porsche, as well as run his own team; he had also been with Rob Walker during the later 1½-litre years. Bonnier again went out on his own with the start of the 3-litre formula, running first – like Walker – a Cooper-Maserati and then a McLaren-BRM M5A.

In mid-1969 Bonnier purchased a Lotus 49B, R8, a former Tasman car that had also been

LEFT Jo Siffert at Monaco in 1968. *(Ford)*

used for the Monaco Grand Prix. He entered it for the British Grand Prix, but it was borrowed back by Team Lotus for Hill, owing to the fact that Hill, like Rindt, was unhappy about driving the four-wheel-drive Type 63, one of which was instead loaned to Bonnier for the race.

The Swede's only start with R8, now painted red with a white stripe, was at the 1969 German Grand Prix, where he was assisted by Tim Parnell's team. It was an uncompetitive outing, for Bonnier was considerably slower in practice at the Nürburgring than many of the Formula 2 cars that also featured in this race to build up numbers on the long circuit. A leaking fuel bag meant that he was forced to sit in a puddle of fuel for the four laps that he completed.

Bonnier's relationship with his Lotus 49 did not last much longer. Again attended by Parnell's mechanics, he got the car going well for the non-championship Oulton Park Gold Cup, fast enough for third position on the grid, but late in practice a bottom front wishbone failure pitched him off the track. Bonnier was knocked unconscious for several hours, although he was well enough to spectate the following day. The car was badly damaged and Bonnier returned it to Lotus, deciding that he had had enough of it.

LEFT Pete Lovely's Lotus 49 was hastily painted red prior to delivery to its new owner. Note the special tool for removing the wheels. *(Ford)*

CENTRE Eventually Lovely's car appeared in the correct white and blue for a US entrant, even if the blue was so dark that some took it for black. *(Ferret Fotographics)*

Pete Lovely

In the USA, the SCCA introduced a championship for what it called Formula A, run, in effect, to a mixture of Formula 5000 and Formula 1 regulations. The Lotus 49 was eligible and veteran driver Pete Lovely decided to acquire one to race in the series.

Lovely's relationship with Lotus dated back to the 1950s. He first ran a Mk8/9, then a move to a Type 11 sports racer resulted in him driving for the factory at Le Mans, and in 1959 Team Lotus also entered him – as Graham Hill's number two – in a Formula 1 Type 16 for the Silverstone International Trophy and the Monaco Grand Prix, but in Monte Carlo the car arrived at the track too late for him to qualify. Lovely returned to the USA and was replaced by Innes Ireland, who went on to record Team Lotus's first grand prix win at the end of the 1961 season. Lovely's only World Championship start prior to his acquisition of a Lotus 49 was the 1960 US Grand Prix, in which he drove a Ferrari-engined Cooper T45.

Having been Hill's team-mate back in 1959, Lovely was eager to acquire a 49 that had been driven by the Londoner. Chapman promised that he could have R5, but the car eventually delivered to him was a Type 49B designated R11, a chassis now known to have had its origins in the 1967 Dutch Grand Prix-winning R2 (see Chapter Five). Before Lovely could get his hands on it, Team Lotus entered R11 for Mario Andretti in the 1969 South African Grand Prix.

With R11, Lovely first took in the two British non-championship races at Brands Hatch and

LEFT Seen here in the 1971 US Grand Prix, Lovely had the DFV from his Lotus 49 grafted to the back of a Formula 2 Type 69. *(Ford)*

RIGHT John Love raced his Lotus 49 not only in South Africa but also in his native Rhodesia. This is the car in the paddock at Bulawayo in 1968.

(www.motoprint.co.za)

CENTRE John Love ran with a bi-wing configuration in 1969. Here he leads Basil van Rooyen's McLaren at the Roy Hesketh circuit.

(www.motoprint.co.za)

Silverstone before returning across the Atlantic to compete in SCCA events and three grands prix, in Canada, the USA and Mexico. Having been hastily painted red, the car was now repainted with an expensive pearlescent white colour scheme with a very dark blue stripe; as the stripe was almost black, it was not obvious to everyone that Lovely's chosen livery represented American racing colours.

Lovely returned to Britain in 1970, again for the Race of Champions and the International Trophy, and stayed on to take in three European grands prix, at Zandvoort, Clermont-Ferrand and Brands Hatch, but only qualified for the British race; he also entered the US Grand Prix at the end of the season but again failed to qualify. Lovely's last two grands prix were in North America in 1971, when he entered a Lotus 69 Formula 2 car powered by the DFV engine from his 49.

John Love

Rhodesian John Love has to be remembered as the man who beat Team Lotus, by one race, to be the first to run a grand prix car in a sponsor's livery. The following year, 1968, he enquired about the possibility of replacing his Brabham-Repco BT20 with a Lotus 49.

On Ken Tyrrell's advice Love bought R3, the car with which Graham Hill had just competed in the South African Grand Prix. The car was returned to the UK before being shipped back to South Africa, where, three months after it had come second at Kyalami in Hill's hands, it was back at the same track for a round of the

RIGHT Peter Parnell at Kyalami in 1970 in the car he bought from fellow Rhodesian John Love.

(www.motoprint.co.za)

RIGHT Dave Charlton, seen here at the Roy Hesketh circuit in 1970, decided that the only way to beat John Love was to join him as a Lotus 49 driver. *(www.motoprint.co.za)*

South African Drivers' Championship, now in the distinctive orange and brown Team Gunston livery. This time it came first, as it would on 13 of its next 28 appearances. More impressively, it was on pole for 23 of those 28 races, the two major exceptions being, understandably, when Love ran in the South African Grand Prix. These successes allowed Love to add to his tally of South African Drivers' Championship titles in both 1968 and '69.

In 1970 Love sold his Lotus 49 to fellow Rhodesian Peter Parnell, who raced it in the South African Drivers' Championship for the rest of the year, with a best finish of fourth place.

Dave Charlton

Yorkshire-born Dave Charlton and his patron Aldo Scribante had seen the dominance of John Love's Lotus 49 and decided that the only way to beat him would be to join him.

Charlton travelled to the UK to find that the car crashed by Jo Bonnier at Oulton Park was available. This car, R8, was rebuilt to 49C specification rather than the 49T layout that it had been using, and entered for the South African Drivers' Championship under the Scuderia Scribante banner. The wisdom of the move was illustrated as Charlton took the first of six consecutive

BELOW Peter de Klerk took over the seat of the Scuderia Scribante Lotus 49 when a Type 72 became available for Charlton. He is seen in the Highveld 100 at Kyalami in 1972. *(www.motoprint.co.za)*

South African Drivers' Championship titles, winning seven races in 1970. That year Love had changed his older Lotus 49 for a March 701, a move that was never going to help him regain the championship, and so Charlton dominated the second half of the season and easily overhauled the Rhodesian. He also took in the 1970 South African Grand Prix with his Type 49 but, like Love, was unable to score against the World Championship regulars.

Three races into the 1971 South African Drivers' Championship season, Charlton secured Lucky Strike cigarette sponsorship for his 49. Meanwhile, Love's March was becoming more competitive but in his search to reclaim his title he then purchased a Surtees TS9. Faced with competing against a 1971-specification car, Charlton also had to think about an upgrade and, after six rounds of the championship, he bought a Lotus 72 with which he was able to secure his second title.

The Lotus 49 was retained and entered for the remainder of 1971 and into 1972 with Peter de Klerk as the driver. A disagreement over engine problems saw de Klerk split from the team after the July Natal Winter Trophy at the Roy Hesketh circuit and, for the last two contemporary races of its life, R8 was driven

ABOVE On reflection, de Klerk considered the Lotus 49 the best car that he drove. *(www.motoprint.co.za)*

by Meyer Botha. This gentleman driver had a major accident at Killarney in the August, a race that saw the end of the Lotus 49's racing career.

BELOW Meyer Botha's first drive in the Scuderia Scribante Lotus 49 was here at Kyalami in 1972. His second was at Killarney where he crashed the car, effectively ending the period racing history of the Lotus 49. Note that the car has now acquired a fashionable air box. *(www.motoprint.co.za)*

Epilogue

The Lotus 49 must be appraised as a package, as a straightforward chassis linked to the most successful grand prix engine of all time. Unlike the equally successful, World Championship-winning Lotus 25 or Lotus 72, there was nothing truly innovative about the car, for the slightly earlier Type 43 had featured an engine stressed to act as a chassis member and bolted to the rear bulkhead.

Perhaps it is in the Ford Special Film Unit's 50-minute documentary *Birth of a Legend* that one finds why the Type 49 has such a special place in motor racing history. This was shot before Graham Hill courageously revived a demoralised team to win the 1968 World Championship and certainly long before Jochen Rindt at last started to win grands prix using the car. The film is the story of the partnership between Lotus, Cosworth and Ford that enjoyed immediate and, dare one say it, fairytale-like success.

That Jim Clark did not go on to win the World Championship in 1967 highlights a downside of the Lotus 49 – its unreliability in its early days. Nevertheless, the Scot won four grands prix that year, twice as many as Brabham's Denny Hulme, who took the title, and was in tremendous form at the start of the

following season, easily winning the opening round of the championship and leaving us with one of motor racing's great 'what ifs'.

In all, the Lotus 49 won 29 per cent of the 41 grands prix it contested. Five World Champions drove a Lotus 49 and two of them made their Formula 1 débuts in one. It was also the last car to be used by a private entrant to win a grand prix. In addition to being Hill's mount for his second World Championship, it also contributed to Rindt's 1970 title.

The Lotus 49 also spanned a period of transition as can be easily seen by comparing a photo from 1967 with one from the car's later years. In its early guise, it was particularly attractive, sleek when seen up against its bulkier V12 rivals. Then it grew wings and various appendages and was never the same again. Even worse, it lost its patriotic and simple livery of green with yellow stripes when it metamorphosed into a gaudy cigarette packet.

It is a cliché to say that motor racing was never the same again, but the way in which Formula 1 is packaged today has much to do with how it changed in the late 1960s, when the Lotus 49 was its greatest contender.

Appendix 1

Lotus 49 specification (1967)

ENGINE:
FORD TYPE DFV 212 8 CYLINDER IN V-FORMATION
CAPACITY 2·993 ccm
BORE 3·375"   STROKE 2·55"

GEARBOX:
ZF TYPE 5 DS 12
5 SPEED

CLUTCH:
BORG & BECK 7¼" DIA. TWINPLATE
SLAVE CYL. GIRLING ·875" DIA.
M/CYL. GIRLING ·625" DIA.
PEDAL RATIO 3·3 : 1

BRAKES:
FRONT DISC } 12·00" DIA. × 1⅛" VENTILATED
REAR DISC }
FRONT DISC } 12·00" DIA. × ·400"
REAR DISC }
CALIPER GIRLING 14/4
MASTER CYL. GIRLING 2 × ·625" DIA.
PEDAL RATIO 3·3 : 1
BALANCE BAR RATIO FRONT : REAR 53 : 47
PAD LINING FERODO DS II

FUEL SYSTEM:
SIDE TANK CAPACITY   2 × 16 IMP. GALS.
SEAT TANK CAPACITY   10 IMP. GALS.
TOTAL FUEL CAPACITY   42 IMP. GALS.

OIL SYSTEM:
MAIN TANK   2·5 IMP. GALS.
RESERVE   2·5 IMP. GALS.

EXHAUST SYSTEM
PRIMARY PIPE   25" × 2" DIA.
TWO TO ONE   4" × 2⅛" DIA.
TAILPIPE   24" × 2¼" DIA.

FRONT SUSPENSION:
CAMBER ANGLE   -⅛° TO -½°
CASTOR ANGLE   3°
VIRTUAL SWING ARM LENGTH   81"
ROLL CENTRE HEIGHT   1·55"
ANTI DIVE ANGLE   3°
KINGPIN INCLINATION   11°
STEERING AXIS OFFSET AT GROUND   2·38"
SUSP. UNIT LENGTH EXTENDED   13·50"
"   "   "   NORMAL LOAD   11·05"
"   "   "   COMPRESSED   9·38"
SPRING LENGTH AT N/L   7·17"
"   LOAD AT N/L   342 LBS.
WISHBONE UPPER   9·50/6·00"
"   LOWER   14·50"
TOE IN   ⅛" TOTAL
GROUND CLEARANCE   3·27"
ROLLING RADIUS   12·00"
TYRE   475/10·30×15

OPTIONAL:
ROLLING RADIUS   11·55"
ROLL CENTRE HEIGHT   1·85"
VIRTUAL SWING ARM LENGTH   94"
TYRE   425/10·30×15

SPRINGS:

	SUSP. PERIODICITY c.p.m.	SPRING RATE LBS./IN.
FRONT	100	97
REAR	110	229
FRONT	105	107
REAR	115	251
FRONT	110	117
REAR	120	274
FRONT	115	128
REAR	125	296
FRONT	122·5	145
REAR	134	342
FRONT	130	164
REAR	140	370

REAR SUSPENSION:
CAMBER ANGLE   -⅛° TO -½°
TOE IN   ¼" TOTAL
ROLL CENTRE HEIGHT   1·55"
RADIUS ARM LENGTH TOP   25·50"
"   "   "   BOTTOM   29·75"
TOP LINK LENGTH   7·50"
WISHBONE LOWER   12·50"
SUSP. UNIT LENGTH EXTENDED   15·25"
"   "   "   NORMAL LOAD   12·95"
"   "   "   COMPRESSED   10·80"
SPRING LENGTH AT N/L   8·90"
"   LOAD AT N/L   669 LBS.
GROUND CLEARANCE   4·13"
ANTI ROLL BAR LINK   7·20"
VIRTUAL SWING ARM LENGTH   78·4"
ROLLING RADIUS   13·25"
PIVOT AXIS OFFSET AT GROUND   5·05"
TYRE   600/13·50×15

OPTIONAL:
ROLLING RADIUS   12·50"
ROLL CENTRE HEIGHT   2·00"
VIRTUAL SWING ARM LENGTH   100"
TYRE

CHASSIS GENERAL:
OVERALL LENGTH   158·7"
OVERALL WIDTH   75·8"
HEIGHT OVER ROLL BAR   31·0"
WHEELBASE   95·0"
TRACK - FRONT   60·0"
TRACK - REAR   61·2"

WHEELS:
8·00 J × 15·00" DIA.   FRONT OR
9·00 J × 15·00" DIA.   FRONT
12·00 J × 15·00" DIA.   REAR OR
13·00 J × 15·00" DIA.   REAR

LOTUS TYPE 49   (1967 F1)
TECHNICAL   INFORMATION
49 -

(Classic Team Lotus)

LEFT Graham Hill leads Dan Gurney (Eagle-Weslake) and Jim Clark at the start of the 1967 US Grand Prix. *(LAT Photographic)*

Appendix 2

World Championship race history

DNQ = did not qualify

DNS = did not start

PP = pole position

FL = fastest lap

Rtd = retired

NC = not classified

1967

4 June, Dutch GP – Zandvoort		
1st (FL)	Jim Clark	R2
Rtd (PP)	Graham Hill	R1
18 June, Belgian GP – Spa-Francorchamps		
6th (PP)	Jim Clark	R2
Rtd	Graham Hill	R1
2 July, French GP – Bugatti Circuit, Le Mans		
Rtd	Jim Clark	R2
Rtd (PP/FL)	Graham Hill	R1
15 July, British GP – Silverstone		
1st (PP)	Jim Clark	R2
Rtd	Graham Hill	R3
6 August, German GP – Nürburgring		
Rtd	Graham Hill	R1
Rtd (PP)	Jim Clark	R2
28 August, Canadian GP – Mosport Park		
4th	Graham Hill	R3
Rtd	Eppie Wietzes	R1
Rtd (PP/FL)	Jim Clark	R2
10 September, Italian GP – Monza		
3rd (PP/FL)	Jim Clark	R2
Rtd	Graham Hill	R3
Rtd	Giancarlo Baghetti	R1
1 October, United States GP – Watkins Glen		
1st	Jim Clark	R2
2nd (PP/FL)	Graham Hill	R3
Rtd	Moises Solana	R1
22 October, Mexican GP – Mexico City		
1st (PP/FL)	Jim Clark	R1
Rtd	Moises Solana	R2
Rtd	Graham Hill	R3

1968

1 January, South African GP – Kyalami		
1st (PP/FL)	Jim Clark	R4
2nd	Graham Hill	R3
12 May, Spanish GP – Jarama		
1st	Graham Hill	R1
Rtd	Jo Siffert	R2
26 May, Monaco GP – Monte Carlo		
1st (PP/FL)	Graham Hill	R5
Rtd	Jo Siffert	R2
Rtd	Jackie Oliver	R1
9 June, Belgian GP – Spa-Francorchamps		
5th	Jackie Oliver	R6
7th	Jo Siffert	R2
Rtd	Graham Hill	R5
23 June, Dutch GP – Zandvoort		
9th	Graham Hill	R5
NC	Jackie Oliver	R6
Rtd	Jo Siffert	R2
7 July, French GP – Rouen-les-Essarts		
11th	Jo Siffert	R2
Rtd	Graham Hill	R5
DNS	Jackie Oliver	R6
20 July, British GP – Brands Hatch		
1st (FL)	Jo Siffert	R7
Rtd	Jackie Oliver	R2
Rtd (PP)	Graham Hill	R5
4 August, German GP – Nürburgring		
2nd	Graham Hill	R5
11th	Jackie Oliver	R2
Rtd	Jo Siffert	R7
8 September, Italian GP – Monza		
Rtd	Jo Siffert	R7
Rtd (FL)	Jackie Oliver	R5
Rtd	Graham Hill	R6
DNS	Mario Andretti	R5
22 September, Canadian GP – Ste Jovite		
4th	Graham Hill	R6
Rtd	Jackie Oliver	R2
Rtd (FL)	Jo Siffert	R7
Rtd	Bill Brack	R5
1 October, United States GP – Watkins Glen		
2nd	Graham Hill	R6
5th	Jo Siffert	R7
Rtd (PP)	Mario Andretti	R5
DNS	Jackie Oliver	R2

3 November, Mexican GP – Mexico City		
1st	Graham Hill	R6
3rd	Jackie Oliver	R5
6th (FL)	Jo Siffert	R7
Rtd	Moises Solana	R2

1969

1 March, South African GP – Kyalami		
2nd	Graham Hill	R6
4th	Jo Siffert	R7
Rtd	Jochen Rindt	R9
Rtd	John Love	R3
Rtd	Mario Andretti	R11
4 May, Spanish GP – Barcelona		
Rtd	Jo Siffert	R7
Rtd (PP/FL)	Jochen Rindt	R9
Rtd	Graham Hill	R6
8 June, Monaco GP – Monte Carlo		
1st	Graham Hill	R10
3rd	Jo Siffert	R7
4th	Richard Attwood	R8
21 June, Dutch GP – Zandvoort		
2nd	Jo Siffert	R7
7th	Graham Hill	R10
Rtd (PP)	Jochen Rindt	R6
6 July, French GP – Clermont-Ferrand		
6th	Graham Hill	R10
9th	Jo Siffert	R7
Rtd	Jochen Rindt	R6
19 July, British GP – Silverstone		
4th (PP)	Jochen Rindt	R6
7th	Graham Hill	R8
8th	Jo Siffert	R7
3 August, German GP – Nürburgring		
4th	Graham Hill	R10
11th	Jo Siffert	R7
Rtd	Jochen Rindt	R6
Rtd	Jo Bonnier	R6
8 September, Italian GP – Monza		
2nd (PP)	Jochen Rindt	R6
8th/Rtd	Jo Siffert	R7
9th/Rtd	Graham Hill	R10
20 September, Canadian GP – Mosport Park		
3rd	Jochen Rindt	R6
7th	Pete Lovely	R11
Rtd	Graham Hill	R10
Rtd	Jo Siffert	R7

5 October, United States GP – Watkins Glen		
1st (PP/FL)	Jochen Rindt	R6
Rtd	Graham Hill	R10
Rtd	Pete Lovely	R11
Rtd	Jo Siffert	R7
19 October, Mexican GP – Mexico City		
9th	Pete Lovely	R11
Rtd	Jochen Rindt	R6
Rtd	Jo Siffert	R7

1970		
7 March, South African GP – Kyalami		
5th	John Miles	R10
6th	Graham Hill	R7
8th	John Love	R3
12th/Rtd	Dave Charlton	R8
13th/Rtd	Jochen Rindt	R6
DNS	Brian Redman	R7
19 April, Spanish GP – Jarama		
4th	Graham Hill	R7
DNQ	Alex Soler-Roig	R10
10 May, Monaco GP – Monte Carlo		
1st (FL)	Jochen Rindt	R6
5th	Graham Hill	R10
DNQ	John Miles	R10
7 June, Belgian GP – Spa-Francorchamps		
Rtd	Graham Hill	R7
Rtd	Jochen Rindt	R6
21 June, Dutch GP – Zandvoort		
NC	Graham Hill	R7
DNQ	Pete Lovely	R11
5 July, French GP – Clermont-Ferrand		
10th	Graham Hill	R7
DNQ	Alex Soler-Roig	R6
DNQ	Pete Lovely	R11
18 July, British GP – Brands Hatch		
6th	Graham Hill	R7
8th	Emerson Fittipaldi	R10
NC	Pete Lovely	R11
2 August, German GP – Hockenheim		
4th	Emerson Fittipaldi	R10
Rtd	Graham Hill	R7
16 August, Austrian GP – Österreichring		
15th	Emerson Fittipaldi	R10
4 October, United States GP – Watkins Glen		
DNQ	Pete Lovely	R11

Drivers' World Championship

1967		
Jim Clark	3rd	41 points (also Lotus-BRM and Lotus-Climax 33)
Graham Hill	7th	15 points (also Lotus-BRM 33)
Eppie Wietzes	–	
Giancarlo Baghetti	–	
Moises Solana	–	

1968		
Graham Hill	1st	48 points
Jim Clark	11th	9 points
Jackie Oliver	15th	6 points
Mario Andretti	–	
Bill Brack	–	
Moises Solana	–	

1969		
Jochen Rindt	4th	22 points
Graham Hill	7th	19 points
Jo Siffert	9th	15 points
Richard Attwood	13th	3 points
Mario Andretti	–	
John Love	–	
Jo Bonnier	–	
Pete Lovely	–	

1970		
Jochen Rindt	1st	45 points (also Lotus 72)
Emerson Fittipaldi	10th	12 points (also Lotus 72)
Graham Hill	13th	7 points (also Lotus 72)
John Miles	19th	2 points (also Lotus 72)
John Love	–	
Dave Charlton	–	
Pete Lovely	–	
Alex Soler-Roig	–	

Constructors' World Championship

1967	2nd	44 points
1968	1st	62 points
1969	3rd	47 points
1970	1st	59 points (also Type 72)

Appendix 3

Non-championship Formula 1 race history

1967

12 November, Madrid GP – Jarama

1st (PP/FL)	Jim Clark	R1
2nd	Graham Hill	R2

1968

17 March, Race of Champions – Brands Hatch

Rtd	Graham Hill	R5

30 March, Rand Autumn Trophy – Kyalami

1st (PP)	John Love	R3

12 April, Coronation 100 – Roy Hesketh

1st (PP)	John Love	R3

27 April, BRDC International Trophy – Silverstone

Rtd	Graham Hill	R1
Rtd	Jo Siffert	R2

BELOW Making the prototype comfortable for Graham Hill. (Ford)

5 May, Bulawayo 100 – Bulawayo

2nd (PP)	John Love	R3

1 June, SA Republic Trophy – Kyalami

1st (PP)	John Love	R3

23 June, Natal Winter Trophy – Roy Hesketh

Rtd	John Love	R3

8 July, Border 100 – East London

1st (PP)	John Love	R3

3 August, Rand Winter Trophy – Kyalami

1st (PP)	John Love	R3

17 August, Gold Cup – Oulton Park

3rd	Jackie Oliver	R2
Rtd (PP)	Graham Hill	R5

31 August, False Bay 100 – Killarney

DNS (PP)	John Love	R3

5 October, Rand Spring Trophy – Kyalami

Rtd (PP)	John Love	R3

1 December, Rhodesian GP – Bulawayo

1st (PP)	John Love	R3

1969

11 January, Cape South Eastern Trophy – Killarney

Rtd (PP)	John Love	R3

16 March, Race of Champions – Brands Hatch

2nd (PP)	Graham Hill	R6
4th	Jo Siffert	R7
6th	Pete Lovely	R11
Rtd (FL)	Jochen Rindt	R9

30 March, BRDC International Trophy – Silverstone

2nd	Jochen Rindt	R9
7th	Graham Hill	R6
11th	Jo Siffert	R7
Rtd	Pete Lovely	R11

7 April, Coronation 100 – Roy Hesketh

2nd (PP)	John Love	R3

20 April, Riverside Continental GP – Riverside

6th	Pete Lovely	R11

26 April, Rand Autumn Trophy – Kyalami

1st (PP)	John Love	R3

4 May, Royal 76 Continental GP – Laguna Seca

Rtd	Pete Lovely	R11

11 May, Bulawayo 100 – Bulawayo

1st (PP)	John Love	R3

31 May, SA Republic Trophy – Kyalami

8th (PP)	John Love	R3

22 June, SCCA Continental 49'er – Sears Point

Rtd	Pete Lovely	R11

29 June, Natal Winter Trophy – Roy Hesketh

Rtd (PP)	John Love	R3

14 July, Border 100 – East London

1st (PP)	John Love	R3

27 July, Taca Governador Generale de Mozambique – Lourenço Marques

1st (PP)	John Love	R3

9 August, Rand Winter Trophy – Kyalami

DNS (PP)	John Love	R3

10 August, Donnybrooke GP – Donnybrooke

10th	Pete Lovely	R11

23 August, False Bay 100 – Killarney

1st (PP)	John Love	R3

14 September, Rhodesian GP – Bulawayo

1st (PP)	John Love	R3

4 October, Rand Spring Trophy – Kyalami

1st (PP)	John Love	R3

1970

1970

10 January, Cape South Eastern Trophy – Killarney

1st (PP)	John Love	R3
Rtd	Dave Charlton	R8

31 January, Highveld 100 – Kyalami

1st	Dave Charlton	R8
2nd (PP)	John Love	R3

23 March, Race of Champions – Brands Hatch

2nd	Jochen Rindt	R6
5th	Graham Hill	R7
Rtd	Pete Lovely	R11

30 March, Coronation 100 – Roy Hesketh

1st (PP)	Dave Charlton	R8
2nd	John Love	R3

26 April, BRDC International Trophy – Silverstone

9th	Graham Hill	R7
13th	Pete Lovely	R11

6 June, SA Republic Trophy – Kyalami

2nd (PP)	Dave Charlton	R8
6th	John Love	R3

20 June, Bulawayo 100 – Bulawayo

6th	Peter Parnell	R3
Rtd (PP)	Dave Charlton	R8

5 July, Natal Winter Trophy – Roy Hesketh

1st (PP)	Dave Charlton	R8
4th	Peter Parnell	R3

19 July, Taca Governador Generale de Mozambique – Lourenço Marques

1st (PP)	Dave Charlton	R8
DNS	Peter Parnell	R3

1 August, Rand Winter Trophy – Kyalami

1st (PP)	Dave Charlton	R8
5th	Peter Parnell	R3

29 August, False Bay 100 – Killarney

1st	Dave Charlton	R8

13 September, Rhodesian GP – Bulawayo

1st	Dave Charlton	R8
4th	Peter Parnell	R3

3 October, Rand Spring Trophy – Kyalami

1st (PP)	Dave Charlton	R8

17 October, Welkom 100 – Goldfields Raceway

1st (PP)	Dave Charlton	R8

1971

9 January, Cape South Eastern Trophy – Killarney

Rtd (PP)	Dave Charlton	R8

24 January, Argentine GP – Buenos Aires

9th	Wilson Fittipaldi	R6

30 January, Highveld 100 – Kyalami

1st	Dave Charlton	R8

21 March, Race of Champions – Brands Hatch

DNS	Tony Trimmer	R6

28 March, Questor GP – Ontario Motor Speedway

DNS	Pete Lovely	R11

9 April, Rothmans Trophy – Oulton Park

6th	Tony Trimmer	R6

10 April, Coronation 100 – Roy Hesketh

1st (PP)	Dave Charlton	R8

1 May, Goldfields Autumn Trophy – Goldfields Raceway

2nd	Dave Charlton	R8

2 May, L&M GP – Laguna Seca

6th	Pete Lovely	R11

16 May, Bulawayo 100 – Bulawayo

1st	Dave Charlton	R8

5 June, SA Republic Trophy – Kyalami

1st	Dave Charlton	R8

4 July, Natal Winter Trophy – Roy Hesketh

Rtd	Dave Charlton	R8

7 August, 25th Anniversary Trophy – Kyalami

4th	Peter de Klerk	R8

28 August, False Bay 100 – Killarney

4th	Peter de Klerk	R8

19 September, Rhodesian GP – Bulawayo

Rtd	Peter de Klerk	R8

10 October, Rand Spring Trophy – Kyalami

7th	Peter de Klerk	R8

23 October, Welcom 100 – Goldfields Raceway

6th	Peter de Klerk	R8

1972

8 January, Cape South Eastern Trophy – Kyalami

2nd	Peter de Klerk	R8

29 January, Highveld 100 – Kyalami

2nd	Peter de Klerk	R8

3 April, Coronation 100 – Roy Hesketh

Rtd	Peter de Klerk	R8

22 April, Goldfields Autumn Trophy – Goldfields Raceway

Rtd	Peter de Klerk	R8

14 May, Bulawayo 100 – Bulawayo

DNS	Peter de Klerk	R8

3 June, SA Republic Trophy – Kyalami

Rtd	Peter de Klerk	R8

2 July, Natal Winter Trophy – Kyalami

DNS	Peter de Klerk	R8

5 August, Rand Winter Trophy – Kyalami

5th	Meyer Botha	R8

26 August, False Bay 100 – Killarney

Rtd	Meyer Botha	R8

South African Drivers' Championship

1968	John Love	1st	54 points (also Brabham BT20)
1969	John Love	1st	43 points
1970	Dave Charlton	1st	69 points
	John Love	2nd	37 points
	Peter Parnell	9th	10 points
1971	Dave Charlton	1st	72 points (also Lotus 72)
	Peter de Klerk	11th=	3 points
1972	Peter de Klerk	7th	12 points
	Meyer Botha	12th=	2 points

SCCA Continental Championship

1969	Pete Lovely	25th=	1 point

Appendix 4

Tasman series race history

1968		
8 January, New Zealand GP – Pukekohe		
Rtd (PP)	Jim Clark	R2
13 January, Rothmans International – Levin		
Rtd	Jim Clark	R2
20 January, Lady Wigram Trophy – Christchurch		
1st (PP)	Jim Clark	R2
27 January, Teretonga Trophy – Invercargill		
2nd (FL)	Jim Clark	R2
11 February, Rothmans 100 – Surfers Paradise		
1st	Jim Clark	R2
2nd	Graham Hill	R1
18 February, Warwick Farm 100 – Warwick Farm		
1st (PP)	Jim Clark	R2
2nd	Graham Hill	R1
26 February, Australian GP – Sandown Park		
1st	Jim Clark	R2
3rd	Graham Hill	R1
4 March, South Pacific Trophy – Longford		
5th	Jim Clark	R2
6th	Graham Hill	R1

1969		
4 January, New Zealand GP – Pukekohe		
2nd (FL)	Jochen Rindt	–
Rtd	Graham Hill	–
11 January, Rothmans International – Levin		
Rtd	Graham Hill	–
Rtd	Jochen Rindt	–
18 January, Lady Wigram Trophy – Christchurch		
1st (PP/FL)	Jochen Rindt	–
2nd	Graham Hill	–
25 January, Rothmans International Trophy – Teretonga		
2nd	Graham Hill	–
Rtd (PP)	Jochen Rindt	–
2 February, Australian GP – Lakeside		
4th	Graham Hill	–
Rtd	Jochen Rindt	–
9 February, Warwick Farm 100 – Warwick Farm		
1st (PP)	Jochen Rindt	–
11th (FL)	Graham Hill	–
16 February, Sandown Park International – Sandown Park		
2nd (PP)	Jochen Rindt	–
6th	Graham Hill	–

Tasman series standings

1968	Jim Clark	1st	44 points
	Graham Hill	4th	17 points

1969	Jochen Rindt	2nd	30 points
	Graham Hill	5th	16 points

Appendix 5

Extracts from FIA Yearbook of Automobile Sport 1968

FIA WORLD CHAMPIONSHIP OF DRIVERS

1968 regulations

Art 1 The classification for the World Championship of Drivers is determined by the results obtained in the principal speed races, the list of which is drawn up each year by the CSI at the FIA Autumn Congress (1968 International Sporting Calendar, section 1).

Art 2 The events retained for the World Championship shall be open to racing cars of the International Racing Formula No 1.

Art 3 The number of events counting for the Championship will be 12 at the most and at least 5. Should the number of events actually organized be inferior to 5, there would be no championship this year.

The 'classic events' mentioned in article 249, note 3 of the International Sporting Code, will be retained by right for the World Championship provided they are organized under Formula 1. The quota of 'classic events' may be completed, within the limits mentioned above, by other Grand Prix chosen on account of their international fame.

The events counting for the World Championship must compulsorily cover a minimum distance of 300km, but must not exceed a maximum of 400km.

Art 4 The promoter of an event counting for the World Championship shall send to the FIA Secretariat no less than 3 months prior to the date of the event and in 10 copies the Supplementary Regulations or at least a resumé of them which shall compulsorily give the following information:
- Designation of the course, length of the lap, number of laps or length of time assigned to the event.
- Opening and closing dates for entry.
- Amount and distribution of cash prizes.

In any case the final Supplementary regulations in 10 copies must reach the Secretariat at least 2 months before the event.

Art 5 Cancelling of an event shall be notified to the FIA at least 3 months before the date on which it should take place, in order to give the CSI the possibility of choosing another event to replace it.

Cancelling of an event with a previous notice shorter than 3 months will entitle the FIA to refuse the entry of the event for the following year, except in cases accepted as 'force majeure' by the CSI.

Art 6 All drivers authorized by their ACN to compete in the events designated for the Championship shall be considered as being qualified by right to participate in the classification of the World Championship of Drivers.

Art 7 Should entry in one of the Championship events be refused by a promoter, he shall make his reasons known within 48 hours to the ACN of the driver concerned, if need be, through the ACN of the country in which the event is being promoted.

Art 8 In each of the events designated for the World Championship, points will be allotted as follows:
- to the driver of the car placed 1st: 9 points
- to the driver of the car placed 2nd: 6 points
- to the driver of the car placed 3rd: 4 points
- to the driver of the car placed 4th: 3 points
- to the driver of the car placed 5th: 2 points
- to the driver of the car placed 6th: 1 point

Art 9 Drivers will receive the points provided under article 8 on the condition of having driven the same car through the whole event.

They shall besides have covered at least the 9/10th of the distance run by the winner of the event. When the 9/10th of the total number of laps correspond to a number with decimals, the decimals will not be taken into consideration.

Art 10 The total of the events qualifying for the World Championship and actually organized will be divided into two parts of equal importance.

Should the total of qualifying events correspond to an uneven number, the first part of this total should contain one event more than the second part. For each part will only be retained the best results obtained by a driver in a number of events equal to the total of events organized, less one.

Art 11 The driver who has won the greatest number of points according to the above articles 8 to 10 shall be declared champion.

Art 12 Should several drivers get the same amount of points, for deciding between ex-aequo, consideration would be given to the quality of the places (1st places, then 2nd places, etc) obtained by them in the events taken into account for the granting of points (see art 10).

Should this first method prove to be ineffective, consideration would be given to the quality of the places obtained by the ex-aequo drivers in all the Championship events in which they have competed.

Art 13 Should the method provided under article 12 prove to be ineffective, the CSI shall designate the Champion according to such other considerations as would be deemed convenient.

Art 14 The driver declared World Champion will receive the Championship Cup and a Diploma from the FIA.

Art 15 As a general rule, in the events counting for the World Championship of Drivers, the entrants shall enjoy complete freedom with regard to makes and/or brands of equipment and materials used for the competition. Said freedom applies in particular to fuel, provided it complies with the International Regulations.

However, in cases where there is a practical impossibility to ensure said freedom – because of the pit arrangements for refuelling, or because of governmental regulations, or any other reasons – the promoters shall have to notify the entrants, as well as the FIA who may if need be grant a waiver of the common rule.

INTERNATIONAL CUP FOR FORMULA 1 MANUFACTURERS

1968 regulations

Art I A Cup will be awarded to the manufacturers of racing cars of the International Racing Formula No 1.

Art 2 For the granting of this Cup, consideration shall be given to the general classification of events counting for the World Championship for Drivers and open to cars of the International Racing Formula No 1.

Art 3 In each qualifying event, points shall be awarded according to the same scale as for the World Championship for Drivers, taking into consideration the placing of the car in the general classification of the event. Points shall be granted only to cars entered with the agreement of the manufacturers.

For each manufacturer, only the car having obtained the best placing in the general classification shall be taken into consideration. Points shall therefore not be cumulative for a manufacturer in one and the same event.

Art 4 The number of results retained for a manufacturer in view of the general classification will be the same as for the World Championship for Drivers (see art 10 of its regulations).

Art 5 In case of a tie, consideration will be given to the value of the placings obtained in the events taken into account for the granting of points (1st placing, then 2nd placing, etc), and counting only one place per event for a same manufacturer.

In case of a further tie, according to the value of all placings obtained in the qualifying events not included among those taken in consideration for their granting of points (one placing per event for a same manufacturer).

In case of a further tie, according to the value of all placings obtained in all the justifying events with possible addition of placings for a same manufacturer in a same event.

Art 6 By 'automobile make' is meant a combination of chassis plus engine. When the chassis manufacturer mounts an engine of another make the car shall be considered as 'hybrid' and the name of the engine manufacturer shall be associated with that of the chassis manufacturer.

In the case of a hybrid car winning, the Cup would be granted to the manufacturer of the chassis.

Appendix 6

Useful contacts

Avon Tyres Motorsport
Bath Road, Melksham,
Wiltshire SN12 8AA
Tel 01225 703101
www.avontyres.com
*Supplier of tyres for historic
Formula 1 racing*

Bonhams
101 New Bond Street,
London W1S 1SR
Tel 020 7447 7447
www.bonhams.com
Auction house

Classic Team Lotus
Potash Lane, Hethel,
Norfolk NR14 8EY
Tel 01953 601621
www.classicteamlotus.co.uk
*Maintains and races own and
customers' Team Lotus racing cars*

Duncan Hamilton & Co
PO Box 222, Hook,
Basingstoke,
Hampshire
RG27 9YZ
Tel 01256 765000
www.duncanhamilton.com
Dealer in classic racing cars

Ellis Clowes
27 Horse Fair,
Banbury,
Oxfordshire OX16 0AE
Tel 01295 221190
www.ellisclowes.com
Insurance broker

Geoff Richardson Racing Engines
7 Brook Road, Bicton Industrial Park,
Kimbolton,
Cambridgeshire PE28 0LR
Tel 01480 861599
www.geoffrichardsonengines.com
*Historic race engine supplier and
rebuilder*

Hagerty International
The Arch Barn, Pury Hill Farm,
Towcester,
Northamptonshire NN12 7TB
Tel 0844 824 1130
www.hagertyinsurance.co.uk
Insurance broker

Hall & Hall
Graham Hill Way,
Cherry Holt Road, Bourne,
Lincolnshire PE10 9PJ
Tel 01778 392562
www.hallandhall.net
*Historic racing car sales, restoration
and race preparation*

Hewland Engineering
Waltham Road,
White Waltham, Maidenhead,
Berkshire SL6 3LR
Tel 01628 827600
www.hewland.com
Gearbox manufacturer

Historic Grand Prix
4 Finch Road,
North Salem, NY 10560, USA
www.historicgrandprix.com
Historic Formula 1 race organiser

Langford Performance Engineering
17 Bradfield Close,
Finedon Road Industrial Estate,
Wellingborough
NN8 4RQ
Tel 01933 441661
www.lpengines.com
New-build and rebuilt engines

Masters Historic Racing
The Bunker,
Lower End Road,
Wavendon,
Milton Keynes MK17 8DA
Tel 01908 587545
www.themastersseries.com
*Organiser of the Grand Prix Masters
series*

Nicholson McLaren
12 Ivanhoe Road,
Hogwood Lane,
Finchampstead,
Wokingham,
Berkshire RG40 4QQ
Tel 0118 9738000
www.nicholsonmclaren.com
Engine build and preparation

Simon Hadfield Motorsports
Blackbrook Hill House,
Tickow Lane,
Shepshed,
Loughborough,
Leicestershire LE12 9EY
Tel 01509 506054
www.simonhadfieldmotorsport.com
*Historic racing car preparation and
racing team*

Index